CW00644404

QuarkXPress 4.0

teach yourself®

QuarkXPress 4.0
christopher lumgair

For over 60 years, more than
40 million people have learnt over
750 subjects the **teach yourself**
way, with impressive results.

be where you want to be
with **teach yourself**

For UK orders: please contact Bookpoint Ltd, 130 Milton Park, Abingdon, Oxon OX14 4SB. Telephone: +44 (0) 1235 827720. Fax: +44 (0) 1235 400454. Lines are open from 09.00–18.00, Monday to Saturday, with a 24-hour message answering service. Details about our titles and how to order are available at www.teachyourself.co.uk

For USA order enquiries: please contact McGraw-Hill Customer Services, PO Box 545, Blacklick, OH 43004-0545, USA. Telephone: 1-800-722-4726. Fax: 1-614-755-5645.

For Canada order enquiries: please contact McGraw-Hill Ryerson Ltd., 300 Water St, Whitby, Ontario L1N 9B6, Canada. Telephone: 905 430 5000. Fax: 905 430 5020.

Long-renowned as the authoritative source for self-guided learning – with more than 30 million copies sold worldwide – the *Teach Yourself* series includes over 300 titles in the fields of languages, crafts, hobbies, busines, computing and education.

British Library Cataloguing in Publication Data
A catalogue record for this title is available from The British Library.

Library of Congress Catalog Card Number: On file

First published in UK 1999 by Hodder Headline Ltd., 338 Euston Road, London, NW1 3BH.

First published in US 1999 by Contemporary Books, A Division of the McGraw Hill Companies, 1 Prudential Plaza, 130 East Randolph Street, Chicago, Illinois 60601 USA.

The 'Teach Yourself' name is a registered trade mark of Hodder & Stoughton Ltd.

Typeset by Transet Limited, Coventry, England.
Printed in Great Britain for Hodder & Stoughton Educational, a division of Hodder Headline Ltd, 338 Euston Road, London NW1 3BH by Cox & Wyman Ltd, Reading, Berkshire.

Impression number 10 9 8 7 6 5 4 3 2 1
Year   2009 2008 2007 2006 2005 2004 2003

v

contents

Trademarks

introduction

This book has a simple goal: to introduce complete beginners to desktop publishing and teach them the necessary skills with which to produce soundly-constructed and well-presented documents using QuarkXPress 4 for either Macintosh or Windows.

Publications on QuarkXPress tend to fall into two categories: either they are over-sophisticated, comprehensible only to the initiated, or they are frustratingly simplistic. By combining simple step-by-step instructions with sound practical advice drawn from years of design and desktop publishing experience, I hope I have somehow struck a balance between these two extremes.

In integrating functions and technologies previously handled by different specialists, QuarkXPress, like other desktop publishing programs, has inevitably absorbed the terminology and processes of many disciplines including publishing, design, paste-up, reprographics and, naturally, computer technology.

As a result of this, great demands are placed on anyone working in DTP today. We need not only to use a DTP program skilfully but also to understand the processes, languages and disciplines involved in its use. With this in mind, I include appendices on typographic measurements, the document-making process and essential technical terms.

Whether you are new to the world of visual communications or a professional in the field, I hope you will find this a useful guide to a remarkable desktop publishing tool.

Please e-mail me at studio@clara.net if you have any comments.

Overview of QuarkXPress

What is QuarkXPress?

QuarkXPress is a general-purpose page layout program, providing the means by which all phases of document design and production can be accomplished. It offers text editing and typographical controls, it provides for the importation, accurate placement and cutting out of images, it has pen tools for drawing lines and shapes, it has automated features, such as master pages and style sheets and it has powerful printing and colour separation capabilities.

The pasteboard

QuarkXPress uses the concept of the 'pasteboard' – the artboard on which paste-up artists in the past created artwork for printing. Pages in QuarkXPress are delineated areas within pasteboards and when pages face each other, as spreads, they share the same pasteboard. There's a pasteboard for each page or set of facing pages and these pasteboards abut vertically to one another within the document window. As you scroll downwards through a document, you see each pasteboard in turn.

You can place items on pasteboards when you work but only items within page areas are printed.

Page grids

You set columns and margin sizes, amongst other things, at the start of a document. These settings define a master page, called Master A which provides the grid for the first document page and for any other pages you wish to create based on this master. Further master pages can be developed from the original setting to create pages with different grids.

You can place repeatedly-used items directly on master pages and these are automatically copied onto document pages. Some typical master page items are headers, footers, page numbers and logos.

Items, text and images

Unlike in a word-processing document, you can't just type or enter images directly onto a QuarkXPress page. You enter text and images into special boxes which you place on pages as you work on a document. These boxes define the area, shape and position of text or images and are analogous to the precisely cut pieces of type matter and guides pasted onto traditional artboards.

Text attributes

You style text using character or paragraph attributes, much in the same way as you do in a word-processing program. You can create style sheets, embodying full sets of text attributes to style paragraphs quickly and consistently.

Automatic hyphenation and the way paragraphs are justified are controlled by H&Js (hyphenation and justification).

Picture attributes

You can specify transparent areas within imported images by creating clipping paths based on an embedded image or a path within a linked file.

You can make modifications to imported images, to some extent, within QuarkXPress, but this work is best done in an image manipulation program, such as Adobe Photoshop.

Lines and shapes

You can make up simple graphic elements using standard text or picture boxes, lines and polygons.

You can also draw lines and shaped text and picture boxes using the bézier variants of the creation tools. These tools allow you to draw editable paths complete with anchor points and bézier handles as in a draw program. Once created, shapes can be merged using one of six effects.

Thus there is no need to create such graphic items in another program unless they are of a complex nature.

Printing

You can output documents on desktop printers for proofing and printing purposes. You can also output documents to bromide or film and produce colour separations ready for plate-making. QuarkXPress will automatically colour separate all imported images, whether they contain process, Hi-Fi or spot colours.

Conventions used in this book

Keystrokes in the main text are shown as icons, such as [⌘].

When icons are separated by a + sign, as in [⌘] [Alt] [Shift] + [Delete], the modifier key(s) before the + sign should be held down together, whilst the key after the + sign is pressed.

Some keyboards include an [Option] instead of the [Alt] key.

QuarkXPress items, such as text or picture boxes, are illustrated as they appear on screen, often with guides and invisibles (non-printing characters) showing.

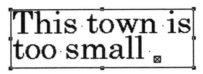

Figure I.1 How a selected text box appears on screen when guides and invisibles are showing

Dialog boxes and palettes are generally illustrated as they appear on a Macintosh.

Other margin icons in this book are used in the following contexts.

- Single-step instructions and key points.

① Step-by-step instructions.

❗ Warnings and critical information.

▲ Helpful hints.

✚ Additional non-essential information.

01

the
QuarkXPress
interface

In this chapter you will learn:
- about the QuarkXPress interface
- about the document window and palettes
- about Macintosh and Windows basics

QuarkXPress interface

This chapter is intended as a general reference to three key features of QuarkXPress, namely the QuarkXPress document window and the Tool and Measurements palettes.

For those new to either the Macintosh or Windows, the final sub-section covers the standard controls used within each program.

The controls on each platform work in a similar manner although their appearance is subject to differing visual standards (see Figure 1.1). If you are familiar with either system you can skip this later sub-section.

As far as the key QuarkXPress features are concerned, you may wish to just peruse the information and move on, referring back to it as and when necessary.

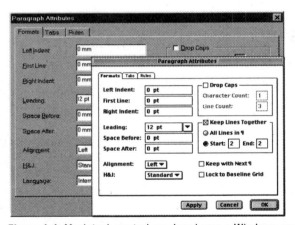

Figure 1.1 Macintosh control overlayed over a Windows equivalent

Document window and palettes

The document window

The document window (Figure 1.2) displays an open QuarkXPress document.

Features include:

① title bar

② close box

③ zoom box

④ size box

⑤ document page, with pasteboard area

⑥ scroll bars

⑦ rulers

⑧ ruler origin

⑨ view percent field

⑩ page number indicator

⑪ go-to-page pop-up menu

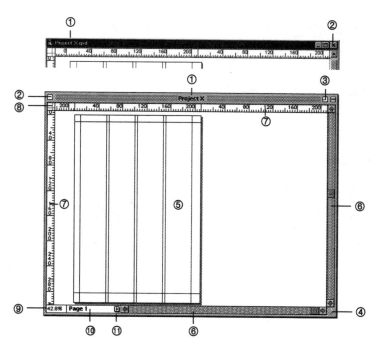

Figure 1.2 Macintosh document window with Windows title bar above

The tool palette

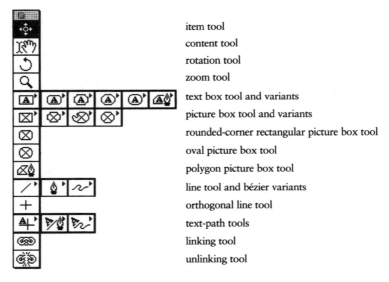

item tool

content tool

rotation tool

zoom tool

text box tool and variants

picture box tool and variants

rounded-corner rectangular picture box tool

oval picture box tool

polygon picture box tool

line tool and bézier variants

orthogonal line tool

text-path tools

linking tool

unlinking tool

Figure 1.3 The tool palette

Using the tool palette

Showing the tool palette

• Choose Show Tools from the View menu.

Selecting a tool

• Click once on a tool icon and then release the mouse button.

The tool you select determines what you can do with the mouse and the keyboard and which menu and menu commands are available.

▲ Select tools sharing the same location within the palette by click-dragging to the tool in the pop-up menu.

The measurements palette

Options in the measurements palette

Text box selected (left end)

Hor. position   Box width   Box angle   Flip hor.
Vert. position   Box height   No. of   Flip vert.
                             columns

Text box selected with the Content tool active (right end)

Leading   Alignments Font   Size
Track/kern   Typestyles

Picture box selected (left end)

```
X: 50 mm    W: 72 mm    ∡ 0°       →  X%
Y: 50 mm    H: 24 mm    ⌐ 0 mm     ↑  Y%
```

Hor. position   Box width   Box angle   Flip hor.
Vert. position   Box height   Corner   Flip ver.
                             radius

Picture box selected with the Content tool active (right end)

```
→  X%: 100%    X+: 0 mm     ∡ 0°
↑  Y%: 100%    Y+: 0 mm     ⌗ 0°
```

Image width   Hor. image position   Image angle
Image height Vert. image position Image skew

Using the measurements palette

The measurements palette is an alternative control that can be used for applying many text, picture and line attributes. Specifications are entered into the palette in a number of ways.

Showing the measurements palette

• Choose Show Measurements from the View menu.

Entering new values in fields

① Double-click existing values (if not already highlighted).

② Type in new values.

▲ To enter pt in mm fields, type in p and then the figure (such as p72) or the figure then pt (such as 72pt).

To enter mm in pt fields, type in the figure followed by m (such as 6m).

Moving from field to field

• Press [Tab]

Selecting options from pop-up menus

Either:

• point to the small triangle by the pop-up menu, press to 'pop up' the menu, drag to the item you wish to choose so that it's highlighted and then release the mouse button.

Or:

• position the insertion point in the field, type in the first letters of the item to be chosen.

Applying specifications in fields

• Press [Return] or [Enter ↵]

Macintosh and Windows basics

Scroll bars

Every window has two scroll bars, one for vertical scrolling and one for horizontal scrolling. A grey scroll bar indicates that there is more content beyond a window's borders; a clear bar indicates that all contents are visible (see Figure 1.4).

Using the scroll bars

Either:

• click the up, down, left or right scroll arrow.

Or:

• click the vertical or horizontal scroll bar on either side of the scroll box, when it's grey.

Or:

• drag the vertical or horizontal scroll box along its scroll bar.

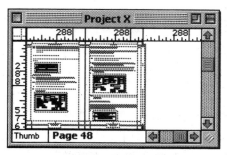

Figure 1.4 Document window with scroll bars

▲ You can set the scrolling performance in the Interactive controls in the Application Preferences dialog box. You can adjust the scrolling speed and enable/disable Speed Scroll and Live Scroll. Speed Scroll greeks (greys) images and blends temporarily so you can move from page to page more quickly. Live Scroll updates the document view as you drag a scroll bar. You can also enable/disable Live Scroll temporarily by pressing Alt when you scroll.

Menus

Macintosh and Windows menus come in two types: pull-down menus and pop-up menus. The menus in the QuarkXPress menu bar are pull-down menus. Pop-up menus often appear in palettes and dialog boxes.

Selecting options from pull-down menus

On the Macintosh

• Point to the menu name, press to 'pull down' the menu, drag to the item you wish to choose so that it's highlighted and then release the mouse button.

In Windows

• Point to the menu name, press to open the menu. Click the item you wish to choose so that it's highlighted and then release the mouse button.

Dialog boxes

Some dialog boxes comprise more than one set of controls.

• Click any tab to display its set of controls.

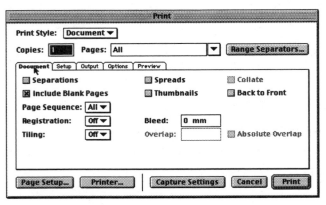

Figure 1.5 Print dialog box showing five sets of controls

Specifications are entered into dialog boxes in a number of ways.

Entering new values

① Double-click existing values (if not already highlighted).

② Type in new values.

▲ To enter pt in mm fields, type in p and then the figure (such as p72) or the figure then pt (such as 72pt).

To enter mm in pt fields, type in the figure followed by m (such as 6m).

Moving from field to field

• Press [Tab]

Selecting options from pop-up menus

On the Macintosh

- Point to the visible menu item, press to 'pop up' the additional menu, drag to the item you wish to choose so that it's highlighted and then release the mouse button.

In Windows

- Point to the visible menu item, press to open the additional menu. Click the item you wish to choose so that it's highlighted and then release the mouse button.

Checking boxes

On the Macintosh

- Click box. An X indicates that it is selected.

In Windows

- Click box. A tick indicates that it is selected.

Clicking radio buttons

- Click button. An emboldened button indicates that it is selected.

Applying specifications and closing box

- Click Apply. The dialog box will remain displayed.

- Click OK or press [Return] or [Enter ↵]

▲ Hold down the Alt key and click Apply to see the effect of changes when the tab key is pressed or a new field clicked. Hold down the Alt key and click Apply to disable the function.

Summary

- **The document window** The QuarkXPress document window has many useful scrolling and navigation controls.

- **Key palettes** The tool and the measurements palettes provide the key means for creating and specifying items within a QuarkXPress document.

- **Using the controls** Both the Macintosh and Windows versions of QuarkXPress conform to visual standards common to all DTP programs.

02

creating and saving documents

Creating documents

Starting a new document

Loading QuarkXPress

On the Macintosh

• Double-click on the QuarkXPress™ program icon within the QuarkXPress folder on your hard disk.

Figure 2.1 QuarkXPress program icon

In Windows

• Choose QuarkXPress from the Programs sub-menu in the Start menu at the bottom left of the screen.

The QuarkXPress menu will be displayed. In Windows a QuarkXPress button will be added to the taskbar.

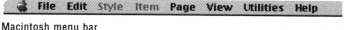

Macintosh menu bar

Windows menu bar

! There is no need to double-click the icon on the Macintosh if it's greyed out as this indicates that QuarkXPress is already loaded on the RAM.

Starting a new document

① Choose Document from the New... sub-menu in the File menu. The New Document dialog box will be displayed (see Figure 2.2).

! If the QuarkXPress menu is not showing, choose QuarkXPress from the Applications menu at the far right of the menu bar if on a Macintosh. In Windows, click the QuarkXPress button on the taskbar.

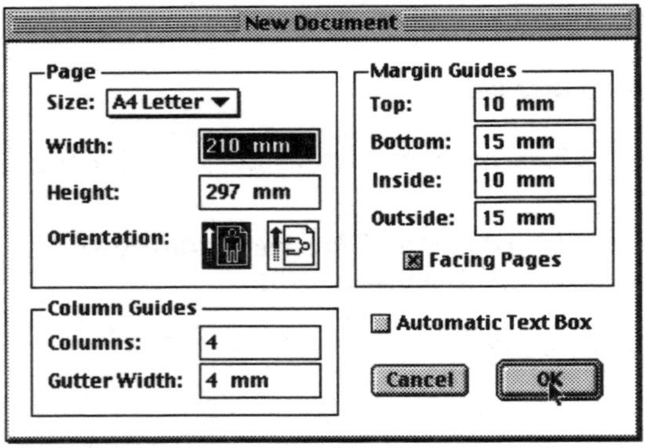

```
┌─ New Document ─────────────────────────────────┐
│ ┌─ Page ──────────────┐  ┌─ Margin Guides ──────┐
│   Size: [A4 Letter ▼]      Top:     [10 mm]
│   Width:   [210 mm]        Bottom:  [15 mm]
│   Height:  [297 mm]        Inside:  [10 mm]
│   Orientation: [👤] [📄]   Outside: [15 mm]
│                              ☒ Facing Pages
│ ┌─ Column Guides ─────┐
│   Columns:      [4]      ☐ Automatic Text Box
│   Gutter Width: [4 mm]   [ Cancel ]  [ OK ]
└─────────────────────────────────────────────────┘
```

Figure 2.2 Creating a document from scratch

② Choose a page size from the Size pop-up menu or enter values in the Width and Height fields.

③ Either: check or tick Facing Pages if your document has a central spine (or fold) and you are printing on both the left and right-hand pages. Figure 2.2 shows the box as checked.

Or: uncheck or untick Facing Pages if you are printing only on, say, the right-hand pages of a document or if your document has multiple folds.

④ Enter values in the Margin Guides and Column Guides fields.

⑤ Uncheck or untick the Automatic Text Box box (in all cases).

⑥ Click OK. The document window will be displayed.

▲ When you are entering values into fields in dialog boxes, it's best to double-click the existing values to highlight them, and then to enter the new value to overwrite them, either including the units of measure or not. For gatefold and concertina documents, base the page size on the size of the document when folded and not on its overall sheet size.

Saving documents

Saving a new document

Before you do any work in your new document, give it a name and save it to disk.

① Choose Save... from the File menu. The Save As directory dialog box will be displayed (see Figure 2.3).

② Enter a document name, overwriting the name 'Document 1'.

③ Select a drive and folder in which to save the file.

④ Click the Document radio button.

⑤ Click Save to save the document. Click Cancel if you wish to abort the routine.

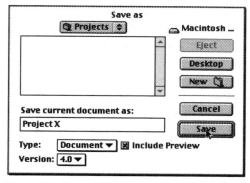

Figure 2.3 Saving a document in a folder called 'Projects'

▲ Resave every five minutes or so whilst you are working on a document, always using the Save command. The Save As directory dialog box will not be displayed on subsequent saves.

Although you can use up to 31 characters in a file name on a Macintosh and even more in Windows, it's best to restrict yourself to around twenty so that names show in full and without being compressed within directory dialog boxes.

✚ In Windows, QuarkXPress documents have a .qxd extension and QuarkPress templates (see pages 196–7) have a .qxt extension.

Enabling Auto Saves

You can specify that QuarkXPress automatically creates a temporary Auto Save file whilst you are working on a document. Should your system 'hang' for any reason, this Auto Save file will survive intact and substitute for your original file which may be damaged. For peace of mind, it's advisable to have Auto Save enabled at all times.

Don't go looking for the Auto Save when your document is closed, as the Auto Save file won't exist. If you wish to check if Auto Save is working, look for it whilst the document is open in the folder in which your working file is saved using the Open directory dialog box.

When you open an Auto Save file after a system crash, you are given the opportunity to revert back to any manual save you made since the Auto Save was last updated.

Specifying Auto Save

① Choose Application... from the Preferences sub-menu in the Edit menu. The Application Preferences dialog box will be displayed (see Figure 2.4).

② Click the Save tab to display its set of controls.

③ Check or tick Auto Save and enter a value, such as 5, in the Every...minutes box.

④ Click OK.

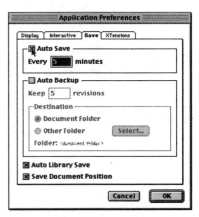

Figure 2.4 Specifying Auto Save for peace of mind

Opening and closing documents

Opening an existing document

Either:

① choose Open... from the QuarkXPress's File menu. The Open directory dialog box will be displayed.

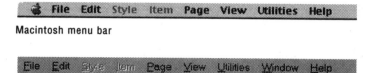

🍎 File Edit Style Item Page View Utilities Help

Macintosh menu bar

File Edit Style Item Page View Utilities Window Help

Windows menu bar

If the QuarkXPress menu is not showing, choose QuarkXPress from the Applications menu at the far right of the menu bar if on a Macintosh. If in Windows, click the QuarkXPress button on the taskbar. If neither is present, load QuarkXPress. See *Loading QuarkXPress* (page 15).

② Use the directory dialog box controls to locate your document.

③ Click Open. The document window will be displayed.

Figure 2.5 Opening a document within QuarkXPress

Or:

• double-click on its document icon within its folder window (see Figure 2.6). The document window will be displayed.

▲ On the Macintosh, folders are accessed from drive icons on the desktop. In Windows, folders are accessed via My Computer.

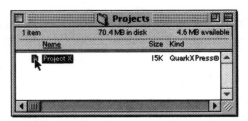

Figure 2.6 A QuarkXPress document icon in a folder window

✛ If QuarkXPress has not already been loaded on the RAM it will now be loaded. Its title and menu bar will soon be displayed.

Creating a copy of an open document

Use this process to create and move to a copy of a document or to create a template.

① Choose Save As... from the File menu. The Save As directory dialog box will be displayed (see Figure 2.7).

② Enter a document name, overwriting its existing name.

③ Select a drive and folder in which to save the file.

④ Choose Document or Template from the Type pop-up menu.

⑤ Click Save to save the document. Click Cancel if you wish to abort the routine.

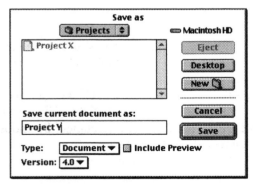

Figure 2.7 Moving to a copy of a document

❗ If you wish the closing document to contain all your latest work, choose Save... from the File menu first and then choose Save As...

! Choose Template only if you wish to save a file for repeated use (see pages 196–7). Templates are partially completed documents, including master pages, document pages, items, text and images, H&Js, style sheets and colours common to all issues of the document.

Closing a document

① Click the Close box at the top left of the document window on the Macintosh. In Windows, click the close icon at the top right of the document window.

② An alert box saying 'Save the new document "Document..."?' or 'Save changes to the document "..."?' will be displayed.

③ Click Yes to save the document. Click No if you do not wish to save a new document or recent work.

Quitting QuarkXPress

① Choose Quit or Exit from the File menu.

② An alert box saying 'Save the new document "Document..."?' or 'Save changes to the document "..."?' will be displayed if your document is still open and recent work has not been saved.

③ Click Yes to save the document. Click No if you do not wish to save a new document or recent work.

Summary

- **Starting documents** All new documents are started by choosing Document from the New... sub-menu in QuarkXPress's File menu.

- **Opening documents** Open a saved document within its folder window or by choosing Open... from QuarkXPress's File menu.

- **Saving documents** Save a newly created document by choosing Save... from QuarkXPress's File menu.

- **Naming documents** Always give a new document a descriptive name, preferably no longer than 20 characters.

- **Copying documents** Move to a copy of a saved document by choosing Save As... from QuarkXPress's File menu.

- **Creating back-ups** Auto Save is not a substitute for manually saved versions under different names.

03

working with pages

Working with document pages

A new QuarkXPress document is based on settings entered by you in the New dialog box. These settings are used to specify page size, orientation, margin and column guides.

The margin and column guide settings define a master page (called Master A). This master page provides the grid for the first and any additional document pages.

The page size setting in the New dialog box defines the document as a whole.

Creating and deleting document pages

Creating document pages individually

① Choose Show Document Layout from the View menu. The Document Layout palette will be displayed.

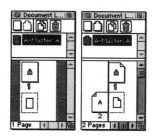

Figure 3.1 Creating new pages in a non-facing pages document (left) and a facing pages document (right)

② Click once on the icon to the left of A-Master A in the palette. The master page icon will turn black.

③ Click-drag the icon downwards into the document page window of the palette.

④ Release the mouse button when the pointer turns into a page icon.

Creating a range of document pages

① Choose Insert... from the Page menu. The Insert Pages dialog box will be displayed (see Figure 3.2).

② Enter a value in the Insert...page(s) field, click on the After Page radio button and enter 1 in the field to its right.

③ Choose A-Master A from the Master Page pop-up menu.
④ Click OK.

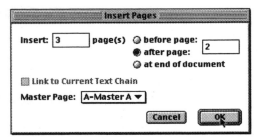

Figure 3.2 Adding three pages to a document based on the default master page

Deleting document pages individually

① Choose Show Document Layout from the View menu. The Document Layout palette will be displayed.

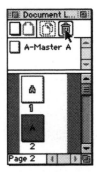

Figure 3.3 Deleting document page two

② Click once on the document page icon in the palette. The page icon will turn black.

③ Click once on the Delete Page icon at the top right of the palette. An alert box will be displayed saying 'Are you sure you wish to remove this/these pages?'.

④ Click OK.

Deleting a range of document pages

① Choose Delete... from the Page menu. The Delete Pages dialog box will be displayed (see Figure 3.4).

② Enter the range of pages you wish to delete in the Delete page(s) and thru fields.

③ Click OK.

Figure 3.4 Deleting five consecutive pages

Moving document pages

Moving document pages individually

① Either: choose Show Document Layout from the View menu. The Document Layout palette will be displayed.

Or: choose Thumbnails... from the View menu.

② Use the scroll bars in each case until the page concerned is in view.

③ Click-drag the page to be moved to its new position. Release the mouse button when the small arrow appears within the adjacent document page.

④ The page will move and the other pages will shuffle along.

⑤ If working with Thumbnails, choose another scale in the View menu to continue your work.

▲ You can click-drag pages from one document to another if both documents are open, in Thumbnail view and tiled within the screen. When you do this a *copy* of a page is moved, not the original.

For gatefold and concertina documents, position all the pages to be printed on the front side of the sheet in a row beside each other. Then position all the pages to be printed on the reverse of the sheet in a second row.

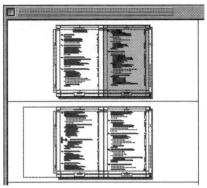

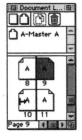

Figure 3.6 Document Layout palette

Figure 3.5 Document in thumbnails view

Moving a range of document pages

① Choose Move... from the Page menu. The Move Pages dialog box will be displayed (see Figure 3.7).

② Enter values in the Move page(s) and thru fields and click a radio button. Enter a page number in the field to the right.

③ Click OK.

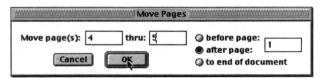

Figure 3.7 Moving two pages

▲ When inserting, deleting and moving pages, unless a document's left and right margins are of equal width, try to avoid moving pages from one side of the spine to the other side, in other words from left to right and vice versa. If a documents margin guides are unequal in width, items correctly positioned on a left-hand page will be out of position on a right-hand page.

Changing a document's page size

① Choose Document Setup... from the File menu. The Document Setup dialog box will be displayed (see Figure 3.8).

② Enter a new page size by clicking a radio button or by entering values in the Width and Height fields.

③ Click OK.

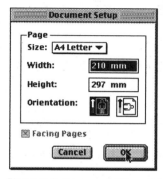

Figure 3.8 Document Setup dialog box

! If you are reducing the page size significantly, move all items towards the top left of each page before changing the size. Otherwise QuarkXPress may not allow the page size alteration to take place.

Changing the column and margin guide settings

① Choose Show Document Layout from the View menu.

② Double-click the icon to the left of A-Master A. Master A will then be displayed. A broken Chain icon at the top left of a page indicates the page is a master page.

③ Choose Master Guides... from the Page menu. The master Guides dialog box will be displayed (see Figure 3.9).

④ Alter the values in the Column guides and Master guides fields.

⑤ Click OK.

⑥ Choose Document from the Display sub-menu in the Page menu.

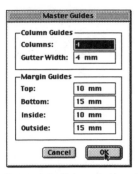

Figure 3.9 Master Guides dialog box

Working with pages

Viewing at different scales

Scaling a page to fit the document window

- Choose Fit in Window from the View menu.

In Windows only

- Press the right-hand mouse button and choose Fit in Window from the context-sensitive pop-up menu.

Toggling between Fit in Window and Actual size

In Windows only

- Press the right-hand mouse button and choose Fit in Window or Actual Size from the context-sensitive pop-up menu.

Changing the viewing scale of a page by pre-defined increments

① Select the Zoom tool (or on the Macintosh hold down [Control]) and click anywhere within the page to increase the viewing scale. Hold down [Alt] at the same time to reduce the viewing scale.

② Reselect the Item tool or Content tool to deselect the Zoom tool (if selected from the tool palette).

Enlarging a specific area of a page

① Select the Zoom tool (or on the Macintosh hold down [Control]) and click-drag diagonally to define the area on the page to be enlarged.

② Reselect the Item tool or Content tool to deselect the Zoom tool (if selected from the tool palette).

Viewing pages from two documents at a time

① Open both documents in the usual way.

② Choose Tile Documents from the Windows sub-menu in the View menu.

Moving around a document

You can move around a document using the Document Layout palette, the scroll bars or the grabber hand.

Moving quickly from page to page

• Double-click the relevant page icon within the Document Layout palette.

Or:

• Choose a page from the go-to-page pop-up menu at the bottom of the document window.

Or:

• Click on either scroll bar either side of the scroll box with the view set to Fit in Window.

Moving a page within the document window

Either:

• hold down [Alt] and click-drag the page with the grabber hand icon.

Or:

• use the scroll bars.

Hiding/displaying non-printing items

Guides, rulers, invisibles and the Tool, Measurements and Document Layout palettes should be visible when you work.

Showing guides, rulers, invisibles, and all palettes

• Choose Show Guides (or other command) from the View menu. If the item is already showing the word Hide will replace Show in the command so there is no need to choose the command.

Hiding guides, rulers, invisibles, and all palettes

• Choose Hide Guides (or other command) from the View menu. If the item is already hidden the word Show will replace Hide in the command so there is no need to choose the command.

Altering the ruler units

Each ruler can be calibrated in any one of seven measurements units. For most work, it is usual to work in millimetres and/or points.

Altering the measures

① Select Document... from the Preferences sub-menu in the Edit menu or press ⌘ + Y on the Macintosh or Control + Y in Windows. The General set of controls will be displayed within the Document Preferences for... dialog box.

② Select Millimetres or Points in the Horizontal Measure and Vertical Measure pop-up menus.

③ Click OK.

Adding ruler guides

Non-printing ruler guides can be added to any page or spread to delineate the major alignments and principal areas in your layouts. These guides are shown in green to differentiate them from the red margin and column guides.

① Choose Show Guides, Rulers and Measurements, in turn, in the View menu. If any items are already showing the word Hide will replace Show in the command so there is no need to choose the command.

② Click-drag from somewhere in the middle of either ruler to a position within the document (or master) page. As you are dragging, view the X or Y field in the Measurements palette.

Release the mouse button when you have reached the correct position.

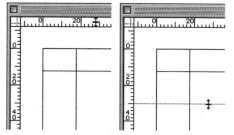

Figure 3.10 Dragging guides one of the rulers

▲ Choose a viewing scale above 200% to position guides with greater accuracy.

Click-drag to a position on the pasteboard to create ruler guides which run across adjacent document pages.

The X-coordinate normally measures from the left edge of pages, the Y-coordinate measures from the top edge of pages.

Margin, column and ruler guides can run either behind or in front of items on a page. Choose In Front or Behind in the Guides pop-up menu in the General set of controls in the Document Preferences for... dialog box.

Moving the ruler zero points

You can measure items from a point other than from the top and left edges of a document page. You do this by moving the rulers' zero points.

You can print large document pages in sections by moving the ruler zero points. See *Printing large document pages* (page 177).

① Click-drag from the small square at the junction of the rulers to a position within the document page.

② Release the mouse button. The zero points will have moved accordingly.

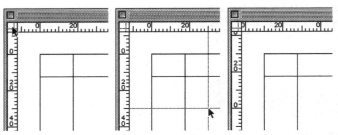

Figure 3.11 Moving the zero points to align with a position on the page

▲ Click once within the same square to return the zero points to their original position.

Summary

- **Managing pages** Document pages are inserted, deleted and moved within Page menu dialog boxes and the Document Layout palette.

- **Working in facing pages documents** Care needs to be taken when adding or deleting single pages in Facing Pages documents.

- **Simple documents** New pages should be based on Master A in documents employing a regular column arrangement.

- **Working with guides** Column and margin guides in conjunction with ruler guides should be used to help you position items on a page.

- **Columns and margins** Columns and margins can be changed within the default master page A-Master A.

- **Moving around a document** Move around using the go-to-page pop-up menu, Document Layout palette, scroll bars or grabber hand.

- **Altering the viewing scale** Change the scale by using menu commands, keyboard short-cuts or the mouse, whichever method is convenient at the time

04
adding text

In this chapter you will learn:
- about working with text boxes
- how to enter text
- about basic text editing

Working with text boxes

Text boxes within QuarkXPress are equivalent to the areas where typeset text is pasted down in conventional artwork. You place text in these boxes which you create on document pages as you work.

The standard text box is rectangular. You can create other shaped boxes including rounded-corner, concave-corner, bevelled-corner and oval. You can also draw boxes to your own shape using the freehand and bézier text box tools.

Text boxes can be linked together so that text can flow from box to box and depending on the location of boxes, from page to page.

Text boxes define the dimensions of each area of text, and their size and position, together with picture boxes, determine the page layout.

Text boxes are often aligned with margin, column or ruler guides for accurate positioning.

You can place as many text boxes as you like on a document page. They can be altered in size at any time and the text within them can be changed.

▲ Although text boxes can be overlapped, it's best to keep text boxes well apart when first working with them to prevent text from being displaced or disappearing.

Creating and resizing text boxes

Creating a text box

① Select the Rectangular Text box tool by clicking once only on its icon in the Tool palette.

② Move the mouse (without pressing the button) over to the page. The pointer turns into a cross hair. Move the cross hair to where you wish the top left of the box to be (marked A in Figure 4.1).

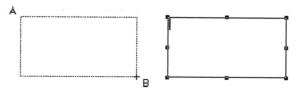

Figure 4.1 Creating a text box

③ Click-drag (press the mouse button and move the mouse with the button depressed) diagonally to where you wish the bottom right corner of the box to be (marked B in Figure 4.1). Release the mouse button.

A flashing insertion point will be present at the top left of the box. When a text box is too small to accommodate any/all text, a small checked box appears within the text box.

④ If a checked box is displayed deepen the text box, by resizing it. If the insertion point is still not present, select, by clicking once with the mouse, the Content tool.

▲ You can use the same process to create other standard box shapes. See Chapter 8, *Working with items* for how to use the freehand and bézier text box tools.

Resizing a text box

① With either the Item tool or Content tool active, click once somewhere within the box (if it is not already selected) and move the pointer to one of the handles at the bottom of the text box. Don't press the mouse button when you do this.

② The pointer turns into a pointing hand. While the pointing hand is displayed, click-drag the handle to resize the box.

Figure 4.2 Resizing a text box

▲ Handles halfway along the side of boxes can be used to enlarge or reduce either their width or their height. Corner handles enable you to enlarge or reduce a box affecting both dimensions at once. Enlarging or reducing a box, with the Command key held down, dynamically alters the scale of text within a box. In Windows use the Control key instead.

After a text box is created, the Item or Content tool will automatically be reselected, depending on which one was in use last.

Snap to Guides provides a fast and accurate way to align items to margin, column and ruler guides. Choose Snap to Guides from the View menu (to tick command, if not already ticked).

Moving and deleting text boxes

Moving a text box or other item

• With the Item tool active, click-drag the middle of the item.

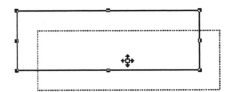

Figure 4.3 Moving a text box

▲ To move an item whilst the Content tool is active, hold down the Command key whilst click-dragging the item. In Windows use the Control key instead.

Deleting a text box or other item

Either:

• with the Item tool active, press [Delete] (the back space key).

Or:

• with either the Content tool or Item tool active, choose Delete in the Item menu.

Entering text

You can enter text into text boxes by using the keyboard, by importing from a WP file or by using the clipboard. We cover the first two methods here. See *Basic text editing* for the use of the clipboard (page 40).

Keying in text

Entering text

① With the Content tool active, select a text box (if one is not already selected).

② Type in text using the keyboard.

If you are unable to see the text and a small checked box is displayed within the box, deepen the box.

If you are unable to see the text because the text appears as a grey line (called greeking), use the Zoom tool to view the text at a readable size.

Entering text, returns and spaces

You will find it easier to enter text accurately with the invisibles showing; the symbols which represent non-printing characters, such as spaces or returns.

Text will automatically wrap when it reaches the right edge of a text box so there is no need to use a return at the end of each line.

Type in upper and lower case unless you definitely wish the text to be in capitals. Capitals can be applied later using the Style menu or Measurements palette. Without a special Xtension, capitals cannot be turned into upper and lower case without rekeying text.

Showing invisibles

• Choose Show Invisibles from the View menu.

Starting a new paragraph

• Press [Return]

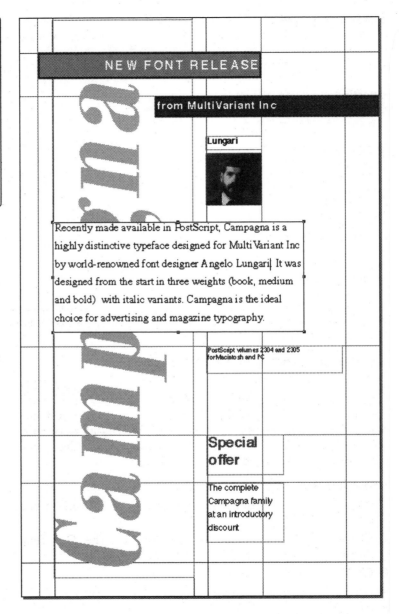

NEW FONT RELEASE

from MultiVariant Inc

Lungari

Recently made available in PostScript, Campagna is a highly distinctive typeface designed for MultiVariant Inc by world-renowned font designer Angelo Lungari. It was designed from the start in three weights (book, medium and bold) with italic variants. Campagna is the ideal choice for advertising and magazine typography.

PostScript volumes 2304 and 2305 for Macintosh and PC

Special offer

The complete Campagna family at an introductory discount

Figure 4.4 An example of a page layout with text and picture boxes

Starting a new line within a paragraph

Use these keystrokes to control line breaks within such text as a heading, address or verse.

- Press `Shift` + `Return`

Entering a normal word space

- Press `Space`

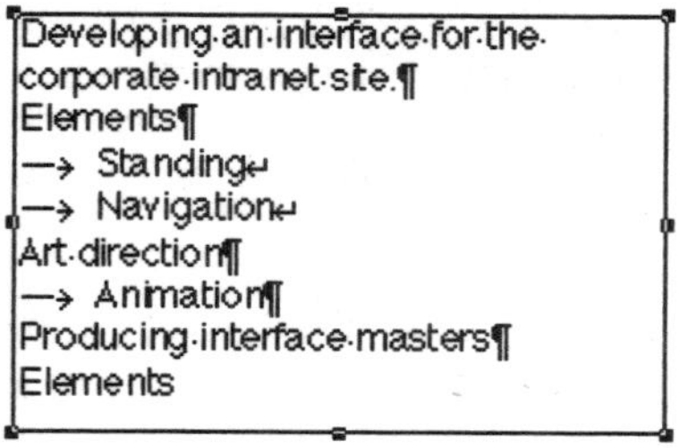

```
Developing·an·interface·for·the·
corporate·intranet·site.¶
Elements¶
—→ Standing↵
—→ Navigation↵
Art·direction¶
—→ Animation¶
Producing·interface·masters¶
Elements
```

Figure 4.5 Use of invisibles when keying in text

▲ Check or tick Smart Quotes in the Interactive set of controls in the Application Preferences dialog box if you wish quotation marks to be typographically correct, i.e. " " rather than " ".

Importing text from a WP file

Text can be imported from most word-processing (and ASCII) files. QuarkXPress imports all the text in a file, complete with page breaks etc. You may wish to bring in only part of a document. If so, copy and paste the text using the clipboard or split the word-processing document into a number of smaller documents first and then import text from each file in turn.

Importing text

① With the Content tool active, select a text box (if one is not already selected).

② Choose Get Text... from the File menu. The Get Text directory dialog box will be displayed.

③ Check or tick the Convert Quotes box.

④ Use the directory dialog box controls to locate the text file.

⑤ Click OK.

❗ Importing depends on the presence of the appropriate WP import filter in the XTension folder in the QuarkXPress folder.

▲ When importing text to be distributed amongst many text boxes, import the text into a temporary text box positioned to one side of the page. Then cut and paste the text from this box into the relevant text boxes. Delete the temporary text box after use.

Seeing all text in a text box

If text is overfilling a text box, a small checked box will be displayed (see Figure 4.6). The presence of this box indicates that not all text is visible. It's good practice to make adjustments to remove the box even if the only hidden text comprises paragraph returns.

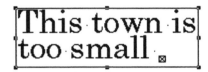

Figure 4.6 The presence of a small checked box indicates text overflow

Showing all text in a box

① With the Content tool active, select a text box (if one is not already selected).

② Either: deepen or widen the text box.

Or: shorten the text. See *Basic text editing* (below).

Or: alter the text attributes. See Chapter 6 *Formatting text* (page 46).

Basic text editing

You edit text within QuarkXPress in much the same way as you do in most word processors. You select the text and then add or delete text using the keyboard and copy or move text using the clipboard.

Selecting text

Text needs to be selected for editing and formatting purposes. Text is selected using the Content tool which is the primary editing tool. When this tool is active, the pointer automatically turns into an I Beam when positioned over a text box.

In all cases, click once on text box to select box first, if not already selected.

Text to be selected	Number of clicks
• Any contiguous text	Click-drag over text.
• Whole word (with space after)	Click twice on word.
• Whole line	Click three times in line.
• Whole paragraph	Click four times within paragraph.
• All text in box (including hidden text)	Click five times in box or choose Select All from the Edit menu.

Selected characters in text are highlighted in colour.

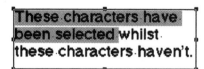

Figure 4.7 Selected characters

▲ When clicking to select text, try to click to a regular beat and keep the body of the mouse steady. If you are unable to click fast enough for selections to take place, select a slower Double-Click speed in your system's Mouse Control Panel.

If you avoid clicking within a text box after you have finished your editing and formatting work and return to the text box later on, the text will retain its selection. If you wish it to forget its selection, click once within the box.

Click-dragging from the right of and level with the last line of a paragraph will select text without selecting the Return mark at the end of a paragraph (¶).

Moving and copying text using the clipboard

Moving and copying text is normally done using the clipboard (a short-term storage area assigned for this purpose). Any text which you cut or copy is automatically placed on the clipboard.

However many times you paste, text will remain on the clipboard until another piece of text is cut or copied.

▲ The current contents of the clipboard can be viewed at any time by choosing Show clipboard from the Edit menu.

Moving text

① Select the text you wish to move, by using one of the methods described previously. Choose Cut from the Edit menu.

② Position the insertion point where you wish to place the text (make sure it's 'blinking' within the text box) and select Paste from the Edit menu.

Copying text

① Select the text you wish to copy. Choose Copy from the Edit menu.

② Position the insertion point where you wish to place the copied text and select Paste from the Edit menu.

Deleting text

Either:

• select the text and press [Delete] (back space)

Or:

• position the insertion point to one side of the text to be deleted and press either [Delete] (back space) or [⌦]

Adding in extra text

① Position the insertion point where you wish to add text.

② Type in the additional text.

▲ If you select text instead of positioning the insertion point and choose Paste from the Edit menu, the pasted text will replace the selected text.

Text within a text box can be moved using a Drag and Drop technique similar to that available in Microsoft Word. Check or tick Drag and Drop in the Interactive controls in the Application Preferences dialog box if you wish to use this technique.

Finding and replacing text

If you wish to change all instances of a word, or set of words, to something else (e.g. change 'the EU' to 'Europe') use the Find/Change function within the Edit menu.

This function can save you longwinded editing work but approach this global function with great care. It's easy, through lack of planning, to alter text incorrectly – creating more work putting things right than it would otherwise have taken to alter the text manually in the first place.

Finding and replacing text

① Either: position the insertion point at the start of a text box to find and replace text in a story (all the text in a text box or series of linked text boxes).

Or: do not select a text box at all to find and replace all text in a document.

② Choose Find/Change... from the Edit menu. The Find/Change dialog will be displayed (see Figure 4.8).

③ Type in the text to be found in the Find What field and replacement text in the Change To field. Check or tick Document if you wish to change text throughout the document. Check or tick Whole Word if you wish the search to be limited to whole words.

④ Click Find Next to find the first instance of the text and click Replace if you wish to replace the word(s).

⑤ Click Find Next again and repeat the process until all instances of the text have been replaced.

⑥ Close the dialog box when finished.

Figure 4.8 Find/Change dialog box

▲ When changing words globally using the Find/Change dialog box, always save the document first. Should you make an error when globally changing text, choose Revert to Saved from the File menu to return the document to its status before the changes were made.

Checking spelling

① Either: position the insertion point within a word to check the spelling of a single word.

Or: position the insertion point at the start of a text box to check the spelling of a story (all the text in a text box).

Or: do not select any text box at all to check the spelling of an entire document, excluding master pages.

② Choose Check Spelling... from the Utilities menu.

③ Click OK when the Word Count panel box is displayed to display the Check (Word/Story/Document) dialog box (see Figure 4.9).

④ A Suspect word will be identified, if any.

Either: click Suggest for a suggested correct spelling. Click on your preferred suggested spelling, if any.

Or: type in the correct spelling yourself in the Replace With field.

⑤ Click Replace.

⑥ The next Suspect word will be identified, if any.

⑦ Repeat step 5 and 6 until all the suspect words are corrected.

⑧ Click Cancel when finished or wait until it's checked all the words.

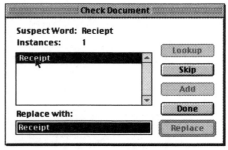

Figure 4.9 'Receipt' suggested as replacement for suspect word 'Reciept'

▲ Choose a view of 150% or above and ensure no palettes obscure the main part of the document window before checking spelling so you are able to see 'suspect' words in context.

Summary

- **Text boxes** Text boxes contain text and define text areas. They can be resized, moved and deleted at any time.

- **Entering text** Text can be imported into text boxes from WP or ASCII files or typed in directly.

- **Selecting text** Text selection methods allow you to select any amount of text within a text box.

- **Copying text** Moving and copying text between text boxes is mainly done by means of the clipboard.

- **Finding and changing text** Any characters, including whole or part words and punctuation, can be globally found and changed throughout a story or a QuarkXPress document.

- **Checking spelling** Spelling can be checked on a word, story or document basis and text changes made globally.

05

formatting text

In this chapter you will learn:
- about basic formatting
- how to format paragraphs
- about other types of formatting
- how to format tables
- about style sheets

Basic formatting

To meet your design needs, all the text you enter into text boxes will need to be given basic formatting, including such attributes as font, size, leading and alignment.

These attributes are applied using the Style menu, whilst text is selected. Some attributes can also be applied using the Measurements palette. See *Using the measurements palette* (page 10).

Applying essential attributes

① Select the text to be styled using one of the methods described under *Selecting text* (page 40).

② Choose a font from the Font sub-menu in the Style menu.

③ Choose a size from the Size sub-menu in the Style menu.

④ Choose an option (if required) from the Type Style sub-menu in the Style menu.

⑤ Choose Leading... from the Style menu. Enter a leading value in the Leading dialog box equal to or slightly greater than the type size. For normal text sizes (9–11 pt), the leading is usually 1–2 pt greater than the font size.

⑥ Choose Left, Centred, Right or Justified from the Alignment sub-menu in the Style menu.

▲ It makes sense to apply any common or dominant style attributes in one operation. Select *all* the text in a box and apply these attributes. Other attributes can then be applied to just parts of the text. You are less likely to leave any text unstyled working this way and it's far quicker.

✦ Auto leading, the default leading value, is useful when initially sizing type, as it self adjusts to suit the font size. However, once you have chosen the font size, specify a value in points, unless there is only a single line of text in a box. In this case, leading is not implemented and you might as well leave it in Auto.

Formatting paragraphs

Formatting can be applied to characters or paragraphs within QuarkXPress. Character attributes can apply to all text within a box or series of linked boxes or to just one character, whilst paragraph attributes always apply to whole paragraphs or multiples of paragraphs.

As in most DTP and WP programs, paragraphs in QuarkXPress are defined by paragraph returns (¶). These returns separate one paragraph from another and are entered using the Return key.

Leading and alignment settings are paragraph attributes, as are indents, drop caps, spaces, rules and tabs.

Some settings for paragraphs can be entered in any one of seven units of measurement but are best entered in points as amounts are often based on font sizes and leading values.

Unless the horizontal and vertical measures are changed to points within the General set of controls in the Document Preferences for... dialog box, most attribute fields within dialog boxes and the measurements palette will be in millimetres (mm) apart, of course, from those relating to font size and leading.

You can enter amounts in points in fields set to millimetres; QuarkXPress will automatically convert the amounts to millimetres. The resulting conversion can be a bit confusing when you later review the settings.

▲ To enter pt in mm fields, type in p and then the figure (such as p72) or the figure then pt (such as 72pt). To enter mm in pt fields, type in the figure followed by m (such as 6m).

Selecting paragraphs

Paragraphs are selected using one of the methods described below, with the Content tool active. If you wish to apply character attributes along with paragraph attributes, select the text using one of the methods described under *Selecting text* (page 40).

In all cases, click once on the text box, if it is not already selected.

Paragraphs to be selected	Method
• Whole paragraph	Either: place insertion point in text. Or: click four times within paragraph.
• Adjoining paragraphs	Click-drag over paragraphs; it's not necessary to select the whole area of a paragraph.
• All paragraphs in a text box (including hidden text)	Click five times in the text box or choose Select All from the Edit menu.

Selected paragraphs are fully or partly highlighted in colour.

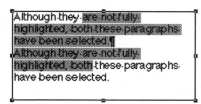

Figure 5.1 Selected paragraphs

Indenting first lines of paragraphs

First line indents are conventionally used to identify paragraph starts except for first paragraphs which are usually set full out.

> **Make·tooth-like·notches**
> in;·form·deep·recesses·in,
> (coastline·etc.).·Divide·(doc

Figure 5.2 Paragraph with indented first line

① Select a paragraph or paragraphs using one of the methods previously described.

② Choose Formats... from the Style menu. The Formats set of controls will be displayed (see Figure 5.3).

③ [Alt]-click Apply if it's not already emboldened.

④ Enter a value in the First Line field.

⑤ Click OK to implement the settings.

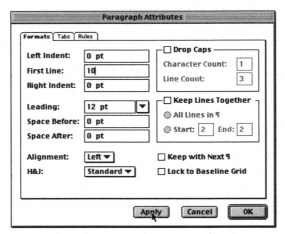

Figure 5.3 Setting a first line indent

▲ Hold down the Alt key and click Apply to see the effect of changes when the tab key is pressed or a new field clicked. Hold down the Alt key and click Apply to disable the function.

Indenting both sides of paragraphs

Left and right indents may be used to reduce the width of paragraphs for many design or editorial reasons.

① Select a paragraph or paragraphs using one of the methods previously described.

② Choose Formats... from the Style menu. The Formats set of controls will be displayed (see Figure 5.4).

③ [Alt]-click Apply if it's not already emboldened.

④ Enter a value in the Left and/or Right Indent fields.

⑤ Click OK to implement the settings.

▲ When entering indents, where possible enter multiples or fractions of the font size in points: For example, if the text font size is 12 pt, choose say 12 pt, 6 pt or 18 pt.

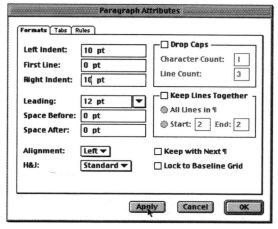

Figure 5.4 Indenting left and right edges of a paragraph

Creating hanging indents

Hanging indents are used for listing work, where numbers, letters or bullet points occupy a space to the left of the main bulk of the text to which they refer.

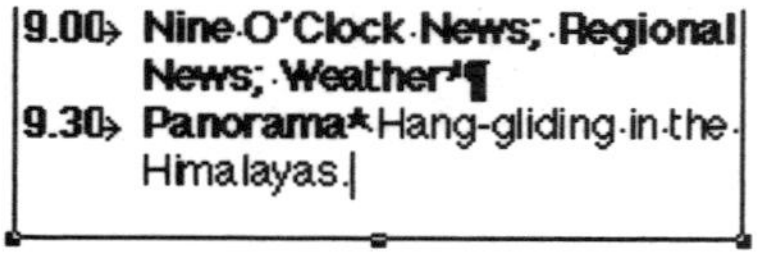

```
9.00⊳ Nine O'Clock News; Regional
      News; Weather¶
9.30⊳ Panorama*Hang-gliding in the
      Himalayas.|
```

Figure 5.5 Paragraphs with hanging indents

① Select a paragraph or paragraphs using one of the methods previously described.

② Choose Formats... from the Style menu. The Formats set of controls will be displayed (see Figure 5.6).

③ [⌥]-click Apply if it's not already emboldened.

④ Enter a value in the Left Indent field (such as 20 pt) and a negative value in First Line field (such as –20 pt).

⑤ Click OK to implement the settings.

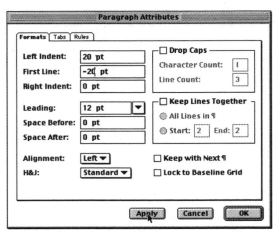

Figure 5.6 Setting a hanging indent using positive and negative values

▲ The left indent acts as the initial tab position for the first line of text. Once a paragraph is formatted it only requires the inclusion of the tab character (using the tab key) for words to align with the left indent.

Inserting drop caps

Drop caps give strong typographic emphasis to a paragraph start, especially the first paragraph in a story.

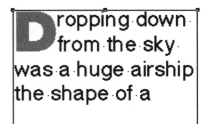

Figure 5.7 Paragraph with two-line drop cap

① Select a paragraph or paragraphs using one of the methods previously described.

② Choose Formats... from the Style menu. The Formats set of controls will be displayed (see Figure 5.8).

③ ⌐Alt⌐-click Apply if it's not already emboldened.

④ Check or tick Drop caps and enter the number of characters you wish to drop (usually 1) in the Character Count field, and the number of lines you wish the dropped capital to fall in the Line Count field.

⑤ Click OK to implement the settings.

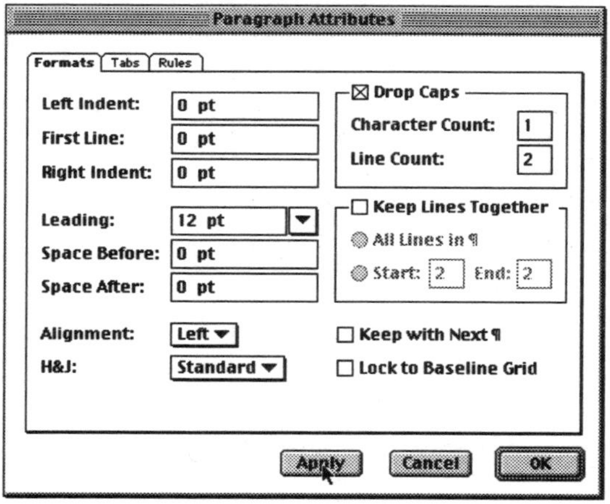

Figure 5.8 Setting a two-line drop cap

▲ Drop caps can be given different character attributes such as font, size and colour. Since a drop cap is a paragraph attribute size is specified as a percentage of cap height and not in points.

Further formatting

Inserting spaces between paragraphs

Use inter-paragraph spacing to reduce typographic density and to create visual pauses between paragraphs. You can also use spaces between paragraphs as an alternative to first line indents.

Inserting paragraph spaces

① First remove any empty paragraphs (i.e. double ¶ symbols) from your text, either by positioning the insertion point within each empty paragraph and pressing ⌐Delete⌐ (back space) or by using the Find/Change method.

② Select a paragraph or paragraphs using one of the methods previously described.

③ Choose Formats... from the Style menu. The Formats set of controls will be displayed (see Figure 5.9).

④ 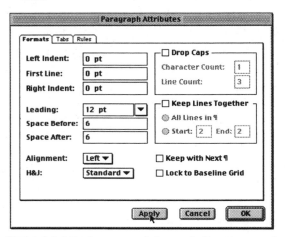-click Apply if it's not already emboldened.

Figure 5.9 Inserting spaces before and after a paragraph

⑤ Enter amounts in the Space Before and/or Space After fields.

⑥ Click OK to implement the settings.

▲ When deciding which paragraphs should contain paragraph space settings, bear the following in mind.

(a) Imagine if the paragraph were to be cut and pasted elsewhere in the text. If you wish the spaces to move with the paragraph, then apply the settings within the paragraph. If you wish the spaces to remain in place, apply the settings within the adjacent paragraph(s).

(b) Be consistent when applying spaces: for instance, if the above guide does not help you to decide which paragraph should contain the settings, always apply a Space Before within the paragraph below the space.

When entering spaces before and after paragraphs, where possible enter multiples or fractions of the text leading value in points: For example, if the leading is 15 pt, choose say 10 pt, 7.5 pt or 5 pt.

✚ Leading is introduced above each line and so a very large leading value will have the effect of visually increasing the space before a paragraph. Neither leading nor paragraph spaces come into force before the first line in a text box.

Inserting rules between paragraphs

Use paragraph rules to separate lines of text visually, to underline a heading or to create a coloured panel under a line of text.

Unlike rules created with the line tools, paragraph rules flow with the paragraphs when you edit or style text.

The trickiest rule attribute to set is the offset, the distance rules are positioned above or below the paragraphs to which they belong. Rules can be positioned using points (or other unit of measure) or as a percentage.

An offset specified in points, or other unit of measure, sets a fixed distance between the upper/lower baseline of a paragraph and the near edge of a rule. If the rule is at the top of a text box, the text will be lowered to accommodate the rule. A percentage offset sets a proportional distance between a paragraph and an adjacent paragraph. If there is no adjacent paragraph, the rule will not be employed; if paragraph spaces are subsequently added or altered the rule will self adjust

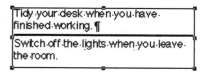

Figure 5.10 A rule below a paragraph separating lines of text

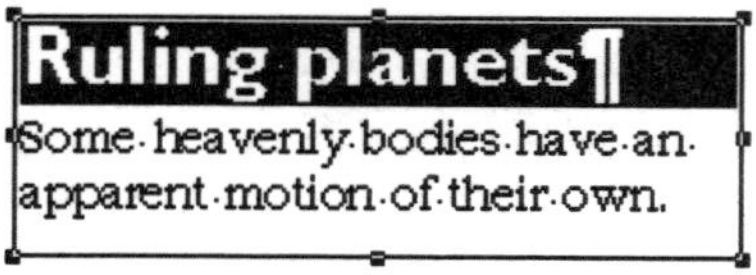

Fig. 5.11 A wide (deep) 'rule above' underlying the heading to which it's applied. Baseline Shift has been applied to the heading to raise it a few points.

Accessing the Paragraph Rules dialog box

① Select a paragraph or paragraphs using one of the methods previously described.

② Choose Rules... from the Style menu. The Rules set of controls will be displayed (see Figure 5.12).

③ [Alt]-click Apply if it's not already emboldened.

④ Check or tick the Rule Above and/or Rule Below boxes.

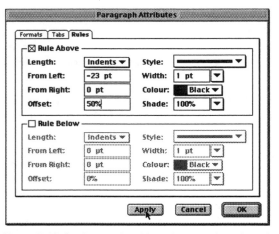

Figure 5.12 Setting a rule midway between the selected paragraph and the paragraph before it

Specifying rules

① Enter an offset value as either a percentage or points value, such as 50% or 14pt.

② Choose Indents in the Length pop-up menu, unless you wish the rule to be the same length as your text.

③ Specify other attributes as required.

④ Click OK to implement the settings.

✚ Indented rules run the width of the paragraph. If you wish rules to run the full width of a text box, enter a negative value in the From Left or From Right fields to match the *existing* paragraph indents values.

Keeping subheads with paragraphs

Headings in text should ideally remain with the paragraphs to which they refer. Otherwise you can spend a great deal of time reuniting paragraphs. You can set up your paragraph formats to do this automatically.

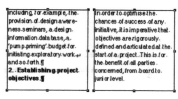

Figure 5.13 Sub-head separated from the paragraph to which it refers.

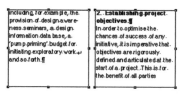

Figure 5.14 Sub-head re-united sub-head.

Keeping paragraphs together

① With the Content tool active, select a paragraph or paragraphs.

② Choose Formats... from the Style menu. The Formats set of controls will be displayed (see Figure 5.15).

③ Check or tick the Keep with Next ¶ box.

④ Click OK.

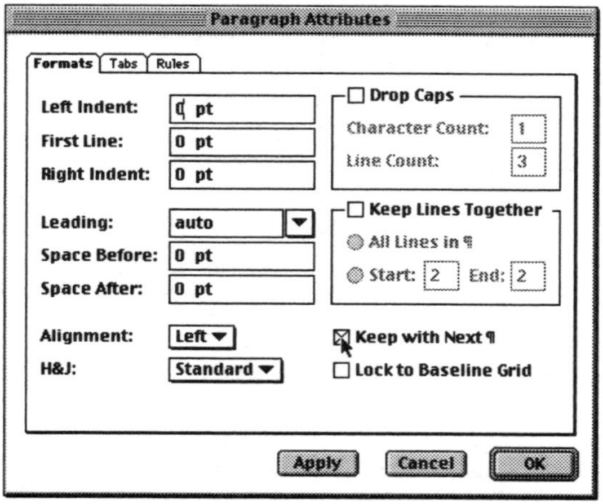

Figure 5.15 Ensuring paragraphs keep together

Spacing words

You can alter word and character spaces to improve the design, copyfitting, legibility or readability of text. The control within QuarkXPress is called Tracking and is measured in percentages of an en space (roughly the width of a lower-case n). Untracked letter and character spaces are set at 0.

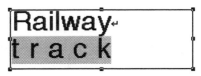

Figure 5.16 The lower word has been 'tracked' for visual effect.

① Select the text to be tracked using one of the methods previously described.

② Choose Track… from the Style menu and enter a figure in the Track dialog box. A positive figure, such as 5 will widen the spacing; a negative figure such as –5 will tighten the spacing.

! The absence of the Track command in the Style menu indicates that no text is selected.

▲ When tracking text for copyfitting reasons, apply tracking to complete lines or, even better, complete paragraphs and use the minimum setting possible. Then tracking won't be too obvious to the reader.

Matching paragraph formatting

You can give a paragraph the same leading and alignment as another paragraph without resorting to the Style menu or Measurements palette. Both paragraphs however must be in the same text box or within linked text boxes for this technique to work.

① Position the insertion point somewhere within the paragraph you wish to style.

② Hold down `Alt`+`Shift` and click somewhere within the paragraph whose styles you wish to copy.

✦ Only paragraph formats will be copied (not character styles), unless the copied paragraph has been styled using a style sheet, in which case the recipient paragraph is fully restyled to match the copied paragraph's style sheet.

Formatting tables

Creating a simple table of contents

You can create a table of contents without needing to resort to complex tabbing or formatting by simply combining right alignment with the use of a single default tab.

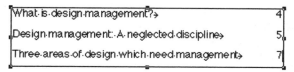

Figure 5.17 A simple table of contents

① Type each line of text using the tab key to separate the text from the page numbers. End each line with a return (¶).

② Select all the paragraphs using one of the methods previously described.

③ Choose Right from the Alignment sub-menu in the Style menu.

▲ See *Creating a table of contents*, page 93 for how to generate a hierarchical table of contents text for long documents.

Creating multi-column tables

Multi-column tables are created by applying bespoke tab positions to individual paragraphs within tabbed text. These bespoke tabs override the default 0.5 inch tab positions which are left aligned.

The Tab key is used to insert tabs within text. These can either be inserted within a WP document before it is imported into QuarkXPress or within QuarkXPress itself.

The Paragraph Tabs dialog box is used to create new tab positions to any one of six different styles of column alignment.

It's important to remember that tabbing is a paragraph attribute; therefore any paragraph can have its own tab positions and alignments. Because of this, always try to avoid merging tabbed paragraphs accidentally as your formatting may go awry.

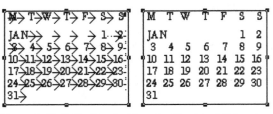

Figure 5.18 Tabbed text with and without invisibles showing

▲ When preparing text for tabbing, reduce the number of paragraphs within a table to the minimum. Use Shift-Returns to separate lines and use Returns only to separate those lines between which you wish to insert paragraph spaces, rules or different tabbing. Always avoid having tabs at end of lines with text wrapping from line to line.

Accessing the Paragraph Tabs dialog box

① Select a paragraph or paragraphs within the table using one of the methods previously described.

② Choose Tabs... from the Style menu. The Tabs set of controls will be displayed together with a ruler attached to the top of the text box (see Figure 5.19).

③ [Alt]-click Apply if it's not already emboldened.

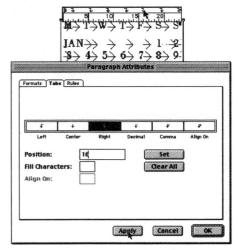

Figure 5.19 Specifying a right aligned tab 16 pt from the left edge of a paragraph

Setting new tab positions

① Select an option in the Alignment bar.

② Either: click the tab ruler above the text box to position a new tab.

Or: enter a value in the position field.

③ The text in the text box will automatically move to the new tab position. If the tab is incorrectly positioned, click-drag its icon to a new position on the ruler.

④ Repeat stages 1–3 until all the tabs have been inserted and correctly positioned.

⑤ Click OK.

▲ If the end of the tab ruler is off-screen, create a new tab and click-drag it right off the ruler and rest it on the edge of the document window. The window will scroll to bring the end of the ruler into view.

✚ As new tabs are applied, all the unseen default tabs to the left of the new tabs(s) are automatically removed.

Removing tabs within the Tabs dialog box

① Either: click-drag a tab off the edge of tab ruler.

Or: click Clear All.

② Replace tabs, if required, and click OK.

▲ To fill the space between tabbed copy with dots (or any other character): select the tab to the right of the proposed fill, enter a full point in the Fill box.

Adjusting the baseline position of text

Text can be moved up or down relative to its normal position within a paragraph. The control which governs its position is called Baseline Shift. Baseline Shift is similar to the Superscript/Subscript typestyle but is user definable. It can be used to 'cheat' the leading – to move parts of paragraphs up or down, when the required effect can't be achieved through leading adjustment. It also provides a means of moving a line of text up or down within a shallow text box as an alternative or supplement to vertical alignment. See *Altering the alignment of text within text boxes* (page 76).

① Select the text to be shifted using one of the methods described under *Selecting text,* page 40.

② Choose Baseline Shift... from the Style menu. The Character Attributes dialog box will be displayed.

③ Enter a value, up to three times the font size in the Baseline Shift field.

④ Click OK.

Figure 5.20 Characters shifted from their normal baseline position

Incremental type adjustment

The following keystroke short-cuts are useful for setting font, leading and tracking in large headings.

Altering font sizes incrementally

- Increase by standard increments: ⌘ Shift + >
- Decrease by standard increments: ⌘ Shift + <
- Press Alt in addition to above for 1pt increments

  In Windows use the Control key instead of the Command key.

Altering type sizes proportionally when scaling a text box

- Increase the size of all the text: hold down the ⌘ Alt + Shift keys and click-drag a corner handle of the text box.

- Alter the proportions of all the text in a text box: hold down the ⌘ key and click-drag a corner handle of the text box.

  In Windows use the Control key instead of the Command key.

Altering type leading incrementally

- Increase by 1pt increments: ⌘ Shift + ' .
- Decrease by 1pt increments: ⌘ Shift + : .
- Press Alt in addition to above for 0.1pt increments.

  In Windows use the Control key instead of the Command key.

Altering kerning/tracking incrementally

- Increase by 0.1 en increments: [⌘] [Shift] + [}]
- Decrease by 0.1 en increments: [⌘] [Shift] + [{]
- Press [Alt] in addition to above for 0.01 en increments

  In Windows use the Control key instead of the Command key.

Style sheets

Formatting efficiently

For design consistency, much of the text in your documents should share the same formatting. For example, within a single document, all your headings should look alike, all your sub-headings should look alike, and so on.

Using style sheets at both a paragraph and a character level enables you to set the overall formatting of text and apply consistent formatting efficiently and accurately.

Because paragraphs in QuarkXPress are a fundamental styling unit when it comes to using style sheets, you should take this into account when breaking text into paragraphs.

As a rule, all the text in a document should be formatted using paragraph style sheets with or without the use of character style sheets, apart from master page items and those paragraphs with one-off formatting.

Try to use style sheets as much as possible in your work and don't worry if you don't get their settings right first time. They can always be amended at any time; any amendments will be automatically made to the text to which the style sheets have been applied.

Creating style sheets

Any text formatted using the Style menu or Measurement palette can provide the settings for style sheets. This method of creating style sheets is described here.

You can create two types of style sheet. If you wish to record and later apply *all* settings associated with a paragraph, including both paragraph and character attributes, create a paragraph style sheet.

If you wish to record and later apply only the character settings associated with a *part* of a paragraph create a character style sheet, e.g. figures can be styled using character style sheets without affecting surrounding text.

Creating a paragraph style sheet from a sample paragraph

① Position the insertion point somewhere within the sample paragraph.

② Choose Style Sheets... from the Edit menu or hold down ⌘ and click on any style sheet name in Style Sheets palette. The Style Sheets for... dialog box will be displayed (see Figure 5.21).

In Windows use the Control key instead of the Command key.

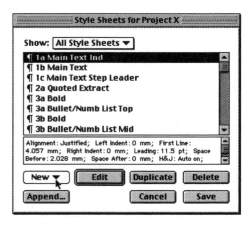

Figure 5.21 The Style Sheets for... dialog box showing the New button

③ Choose ¶ Paragraph from the New button sub-menu. The Edit Paragraph Style Sheet dialog box will be displayed (see Figure 5.22).

④ Enter a name for the new style sheet in the Name field.

⑤ Click the pointer in the Keyboard Equivalent field and press a number from the numeric key pad on the keyboard. This step is optional.

⑥ Click OK. The new style sheet will now be listed in the Style Sheets listing.

⑦ Click OK.

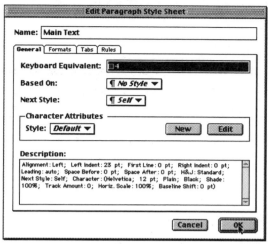

Figure 5.22 Naming and specifying a keyboard shortcut for new style sheet

▲ A style sheet's name can describe a paragraph's function, such as 'Table Heading' or describe its specification, such as 'Times 12pt, Space After'. Numbered names, such as '1 Heading' will be numerically ordered in the Style Sheet sub-menu and Style Sheet palette. Others will appear alphabetically.

Creating a character style sheet from sample text

① Position the insertion point somewhere within the sample text.

② Choose Style Sheets... from the Edit menu or hold down ⌘ and click on any style sheet name in the Style Sheets palette. The Style Sheets for... dialog box will be displayed (see Figure 5.23).

In Windows use the Control key instead of the Command key.

③ Choose A Character from the New button sub-menu. The Edit Character Style Sheet dialog box will be displayed.

④ Enter a name for the new style sheet in the Name field.

⑤ Click the pointer in the Keyboard Equivalent field and press a number from the numeric key pad on the keyboard. This optional step enables you to apply style sheets using keystrokes.

⑥ Click OK. The new style sheet will now be listed in the Style Sheets listing.

⑦ Click OK.

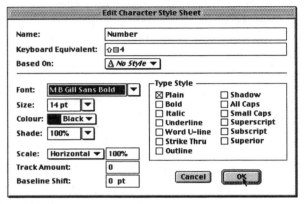

Figure 5.23 Creating a new character style sheet

Applying style sheets

Once style sheets have been made, they can be applied to text using one of three methods:

• Using the Style menu
• Using the Style Sheets palette
• Using the keypad

! When character style sheets are applied to text, a + sign appears after the name of the paragraph style sheet associated with the text. This indicates that further formatting has been applied. This + sign will only appear if the insertion point is positioned within the 'character formatted' part of the text or if the whole of the paragraph is highlighted.

Applying style sheets using the Style menu

① Select the text you wish to style.

② Choose a style sheet in the Style Sheets sub-menu in Style menu.

Applying style sheets using the Style Sheets palette

① Select the text you wish to style.

② Choose Show Style Sheets from the View menu to display the Style Sheets palette (see Figure 5.24).

③ Click on a style sheet name in the palette. Use the palette scroll bars if the name of the style sheet is out of view.

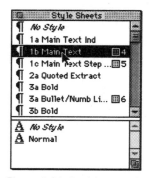

Figure 5.24 Applying a style sheet within the Style palette

Applying style sheets using the keypad

① Select the text you wish to style.

② Press the appropriate number in the numeric keypad.

! This method can only be used if a Keyboard Equivalent is entered in the Edit Style Sheet dialog box.

! Text that provides the specification for a style sheet is not automatically under the influence of the style sheet, although it will look correct. Ensure you apply style sheets to this text as well.

Adding 'local' formatting to paragraphs

You can apply further 'local' formatting to any text formatted by either type of style sheet. Such local formatting can include both character and paragraph attributes and is applied using the Style menu or Measurements palette in the usual way.

A + sign after the name of a style sheet within the Style Sheets palette indicates that further formatting has been applied. This + sign will only show if the insertion point is positioned within the locally formatted part of the text or if the whole of the paragraph is highlighted.

Retaining character attributes

If another style sheet is applied to a paragraph which has further formatting, the further formatting will normally be retained, unless you hold down [Alt] when the new style sheet is selected within the palette.

If another style sheet is applied to a paragraph which has a character style sheet in force, it will remain in force, unless you hold down [Alt] when the new paragraph style sheet is selected within the palette.

Basing style sheets on existing style sheets

You can base a style sheet on another existing style sheet for design consistency and to speed your work. For instance, the style sheet for an italicized version of your main text can be based on the style sheet for your main text. One major advantage of basing new style sheets on existing style sheets is that if you wish to change the original style sheet, all the style sheets which are based on it automatically change as well.

① Choose Style Sheets... from the Edit menu or hold down [⌘] and click on the name of the style sheet in the Style Sheets palette. The Style Sheets for... dialog box will be displayed.

In Windows use the Control key instead of the Command key.

② Choose either ¶ Paragraph or **A** Character from the New button sub-menu. The Edit Paragraph or Character Style Sheet dialog box will be displayed.

③ Choose the style sheet on which you wish to base the new style sheet in the Based On pop-up menu. Enter a name for the style sheet in the Name field.

④ Click the Formats, Tabs and Rules tabs in turn and Edit (under Character Attributes) to access their respective dialog boxes.

⑤ Make any changes within the dialog boxes in the usual way.

⑥ Click OK to return to the Style Sheets for... dialog box. Notice the revised description of the style sheet at the bottom of the appropriate dialog box.

⑦ Click Save.

Amending style sheets

① Choose Style Sheets... from the Edit menu or hold down 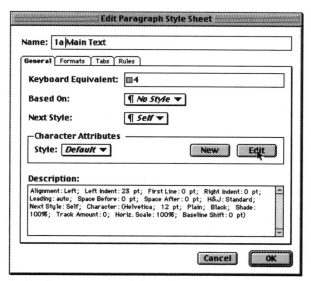⌘ and click on the style sheet name in the Style Sheets palette. The Style Sheets for... dialog box will be displayed.

In Windows use the Control key instead of the Command key.

② Click on the name of the style sheet to be edited (if it is not already selected) and click Edit. The Edit Paragraph Style Sheet dialog box will be displayed (see Figure 5.25).

③ Click the Formats, Tabs and Rules tabs in turn and Edit (under Character Attributes) to access their respective dialog boxes.

④ Make any changes within the dialog boxes in the usual way. Click OK to close the Character Attributes dialog box, click OK again to return to the Style Sheets for... dialog box.

⑤ Click Save.

Figure 5.25 Accessing the character settings of a style sheet

Copying style sheets from other documents

Style sheets you create and use in one document can be copied into other documents. Provided the names of copied style sheets do not clash with the names of existing style sheets, the process is fairly straightforward.

Either:

① Choose Style Sheets... from the Edit menu or hold down [⌘] and click on the name of any style sheet in the Style Sheets palette. The Style Sheets dialog box will be displayed.

In Windows use the Control key instead of the Command key.

② Click Append... Use the directory dialog box controls to locate the QuarkXPress document containing the style sheets you wish to copy.

③ Click Open. The Append Style Sheets dialog box will be displayed.

④ Either: click Include All. All the style sheets in the Available list will be added to the Including list.

Or: select a style sheet you wish to include in the Available list and click the Arrow to the right of the box to add it to the Including list. Repeat for any other style sheet you wish to add.

⑤ Click OK and click Save.

Or:

Copy and paste a paragraph under the influence of the style sheet you wish to copy from one document to another, using the clipboard. See *Moving and copying text using the clipboard* (page 41).

❗ If H&J settings (see page 155) differ between documents, it's necessary to copy the H&Js from the document containing the style sheets first. The process is similar to copying style sheets except the Append... button is accessed in the H&Js for... dialog box.

Disconnecting style sheets

You can unlink a style sheet from a paragraph, yet retain its formatting. Do this if you're happy with the formatting of a paragraph but don't wish it to be affected by any future style sheet amendments. Also do this if you wish to copy a paragraph from another document, and you don't wish its style sheet to copied along with it.

• Apply No Style by one of the methods described previously (see Figure 5.5).

Summary

• **Formatting levels** Text is formatted at either a character or paragraph level.

• **Formatting controls** Apart from rules, most paragraph attributes can be applied within the Formats set of controls.

• **Horizontal rules** Rules specified as part of a paragraph's formatting, move with the paragraphs to which they belong.

• **Drop caps** Although specified at a paragraph level, drop caps can be resized and given alternative character attributes.

• **Formatting a table of contents** Simple contents tables can be created without special tabbing.

• **Working efficiently** Style sheets enable you to apply formatting efficiently, accurately and consistently.

06

working with text boxes

In this chapter you will learn:
- how to alter the layout of boxes
- about overlapping and linking boxes

The adept use of text boxes provides the key to effective page layout. In addition to defining simple text areas, text boxes can be divided into multiple columns, linked together, layered to create interesting type effects, and given coloured backgrounds and borders. In a sense, text boxes are like miniature pages with their own internal and external attributes.

Altering the layout of boxes

Creating multi-columned text boxes

You can easily divide the text area within text boxes into multiple linked columns. This feature is particularly useful when you wish to create a text area with a common coloured background, with or without a border.

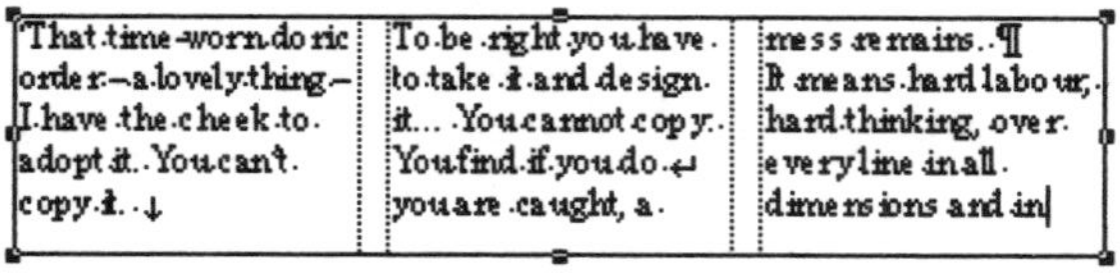

Figure 6.1 A multi-columned text box

Adding extra columns to a text box

① With either the Item tool or Content tool active, select a text box.

② Choose Modify... from the Item menu. The Modify dialog box will be displayed (see Figure 6.2).

③ Click the Text tab.

④ Enter values in the Columns and Gutter Width fields.

⑤ Click OK.

⑥ Enter text into the text box. Provided sufficient text is entered, the text will automatically flow from one column to the next column.

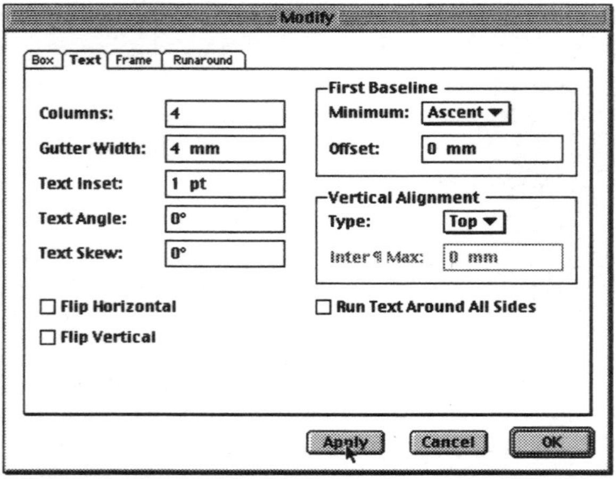

Modify

Box | **Text** | Frame | Runaround

Columns: | 4

Gutter Width: | 4 mm

Text Inset: | 1 pt

Text Angle: | 0°

Text Skew: | 0°

☐ Flip Horizontal
☐ Flip Vertical

─First Baseline─
Minimum: | Ascent ▾

Offset: | 0 mm

─Vertical Alignment─
Type: | Top ▾

Inter ¶ Max: | 0 mm

☐ Run Text Around All Sides

[Apply]   [Cancel]   [OK]

Figure 6.2 Specifying multiple columns and a gutter width

▲ You can force text into the next column by positioning the insertion point before the text you wish to move and pressing the Enter key.

Altering margins within text boxes

You may wish to move text away from the inner edge of a text box for a number of reasons.

• To create a margin between a box frame and the edge of text.

In the arts, space has become an increasingly important concept with the development of ABSTRACT ART.

Figure 6.3 Text inset from the inner edges of a box frame

• To create a space above the first line of text, unattainable through paragraph formatting.

Figure 6.4 Text starting at a fixed distance from the top edge of a box

- To create a text margin within a coloured box

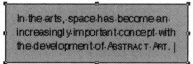

Figure 6.5 Text inset from the inner edges of a coloured box

The control which governs the margins within a text box is called Text Inset. The default text inset is 1 pt and it applies to all four sides of a text box.

The control which governs the distance of the first baseline of text from the top edge of a box (or the inner edge of a frame) is called First Baseline.

Widening the inner margins

① With either the Item tool or Content tool active, select a text box.

② Choose Modify... from the Item menu. The Modify dialog box will be displayed.

③ Click the Text tab.

④ Enter a value in the Text Inset field.

⑤ Click OK.

Lowering the position of the first baseline of text

① With either the Item tool or Content tool active, select a text box.

② Choose Modify... from the Item menu. The Modify dialog box will be displayed (see Figure 6.6).

③ Click the Text tab.

④ Enter a value equal to or larger than the font size in the Offset field under First Baseline.

⑤ Click OK.

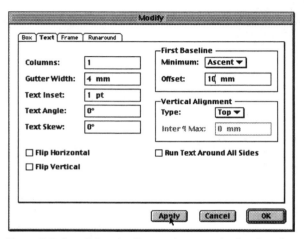

Figure 6.6 Specifying the distance between the first baseline of type and the top of a box

Altering the alignment of text within text boxes

Text within a text box is normally aligned to the top of a box. You can align text to the bottom of a box; this option is useful for text boxes containing footnotes.

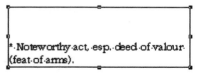

Figure 6.7 Text vertically aligned to the bottom of a box

You can also range text from the centre of a text box giving equal space above and below; this option is especially useful when positioning text, such as headings and quotations, in coloured text boxes.

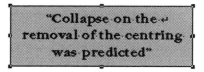

"Collapse on the ⏎
removal of the centring
was predicted"

Figure 6.8 Text vertically centred within a box

Finally you can justify text vertically; this option, which is normally used to equalize long column lengths of text, overrides leading settings, spacing out the lines of text to fill the depth of a text box.

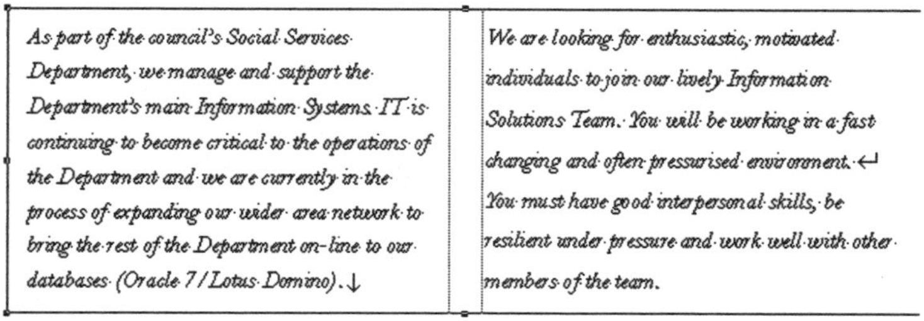

As part of the council's Social Services Department, we manage and support the Department's main Information Systems. IT is continuing to become critical to the operations of the Department and we are currently in the process of expanding our wider area network to bring the rest of the Department on-line to our databases (Oracle 7 / Lotus Domino). ↓

We are looking for enthusiastic, motivated individuals to join our lively Information Solutions Team. You will be working in a fast changing and often pressurised environment. ⏎ You must have good interpersonal skills, be resilient under pressure and work well with other members of the team.

Figure 6.9 Text vertically justified within a box

Altering the vertical alignment

① With either the Item tool or Content tool active, select a text box.

② Choose Modify... from the Item menu. The Modify dialog box will be displayed (see Figure 6.10).

③ Click the Text tab.

④ Choose an option in the Vertical Alignment, Type pop-up menu.

⑤ Click OK.

✦ Vertical Alignment Justified is often used to 'stretch out' text in the absence of sufficient copy. It overrides leading settings and for this reason you may prefer to avoid the technique. Its effect on leading can be minimized by entering a value, such as 3 mm, in the Inter ¶ Max field. This field is only available when Justified is chosen.

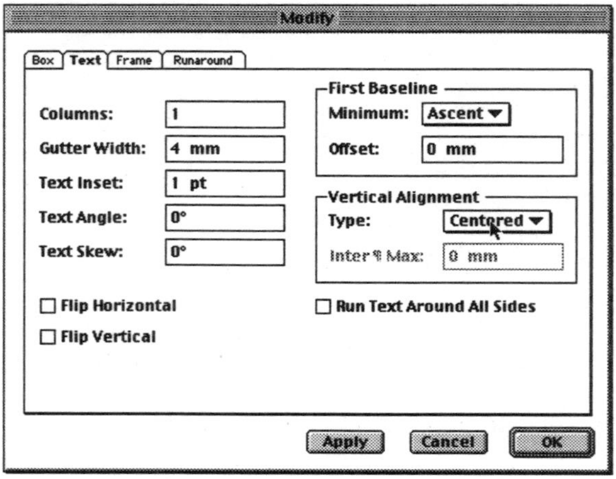

Figure 6.10 Centring text vertically within a box

Overlapping and linking boxes

Layering text

You can overlay text to create typographic effects with a sense of depth. Normally when a text box is placed above another text box, text in the underlying box is displaced. The control which causes this effect is called Runaround and it needs to be disabled for the text to remain in place.

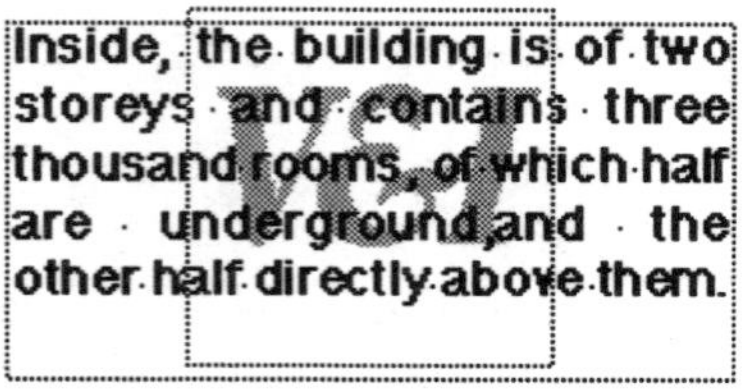

Figure 6.11 Overlayed type using two text boxes

① With either the Item tool or Content tool active, select the overlaying text box.

② Choose Runaround... from the Item menu. The Runaround set of controls will be displayed (see Figure 6.6).

③ Choose None from the Type pop-up menu.

④ Click OK.

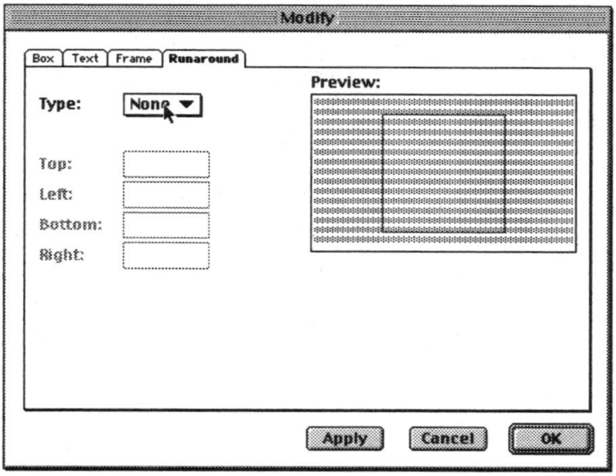

Figure 6.12 Specifying a clear background for a text box

▲ See Chapter 8, *Working with items* for how to alter the stacking order of items.

✦ Text boxes with the Runaround type set to None will automatically become transparent if the box had previously a 0% shaded or White background.

Linking text boxes

You can link any number of text boxes together so that text flows from box to box. The boxes can either be single column or multi-column, it makes no difference. Linking is particularly useful when text needs to run across many columns of varying height and you wish to keep the text in one piece for ease of editing.

The process of linking is straightforward provided you take care only to click within the text boxes you intend to link and that you click the boxes in the order you wish the text to flow.

Linking two text boxes

① Select the Linking tool in the Tools palette.

② Move the pointer over the first text box and click once and then move the pointer over the second text box and click once again.

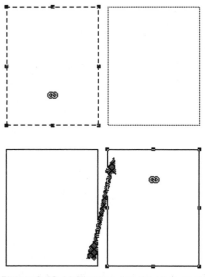

Figure 6.13 Linking two boxes: click on the first box (top) and then click on the second box (bottom)

Unlinking two text boxes

① With either the Item tool or Content tool active, select one of the linked text boxes.

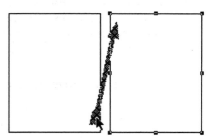

Figure 6.14 Unlinking two boxes: just click on the tailfeather

② Select the Unlinking tool in the Tools palette. An arrow will be displayed linking one box to the next.

③ Move the pointer over the arror's tailfeather and click once.

Linking more than two text boxes at a time

① Hold down [Alt] and select the Linking tool in the Tools palette. Release [Alt] and the mouse button.

② Move the pointer over the first text box and click once, move the pointer over the second text box and click once again, move the pointer over the third text box and click once again and so on.

③ Turn off the Linking tool by selecting the Item or Content tool.

Unlinking more than two text boxes at a time

① With either the Item tool or Content active, select one of the linked text boxes.

② Hold down [Alt] and select the Unlinking tool in the Tools palette. Release [Alt] and the mouse button. Arrows will be displayed linking the boxes together.

③ Move the pointer over the tailfeather of the final arrow and click once, move the pointer over the tailfeather of the arrow before it and click once again and so on.

Re-routing text

① Hold down [Alt] and select the Linking tool in the Tools palette. Release [Alt] and the mouse button.

② Move the pointer over the text box from which you wish to re-route the text and click once, move the pointer over the text box to which you wish to route the text and click once again, move the pointer over the next text box and click once again and so on.

③ Turn off the Linking tool by selecting the Item tool or Content tool.

✦ You will notice in the previous steps that the Alt key is used for multiple
linkages. The role of the Alt key is to keep the Linking and Unlinking tools
active. If this key is used, it is important to select the Item or Content tool
immediately after you have completed the process, to turn either tool off.

Summary

- **Use of boxes** The adept use of text boxes provides the key to
effective page layout.
- **Text attributes** The text inset of boxes can be modified along
with the number of columns and their gutter width.
- **Vertical alignment** The vertical alignment of text can be modified to equalize column heights and to range display text vertically within coloured and/or framed panels.
- **Linking boxes** Linked and multi-column text boxes enable
long pieces of text to be kept together for ease of editing.
- **Overlaying text** Text in different boxes to be overlaid to give
depth to a layout.

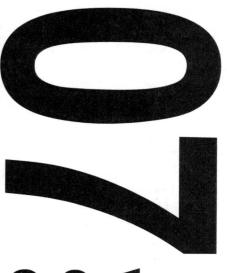

07

working with complex documents

In this chapter you will learn:

- how to use master pages
- about page numbering
- how to add other master pages
- how to link documents
- how to create a table of contents
- how to make an index

Using master pages

In multi-page documents, there is likely to be some text that appears on all or most pages; headers (running heads), footers and folios (page numbers) are typical examples of such items. Fortunately there is no need for you to enter such items on every page. To do so would be time-consuming and inconsistencies will inevitably creep in however carefully you worked.

The easiest way to enter such items, and to ensure consistency, is to use master pages. The default master page is Master A and its icon can be viewed in the Document Layout palette.

Master A already provides each document page with the blue margin and column guides. Place items at any time on this master page and they will automatically be copied onto document pages as if you had created them on each page individually.

You can modify master page items on a document page without affecting the originals on the master page itself.

Adding master page items

Opening Master A

① Choose Document Layout from the View menu. The Document Layout palette will be displayed (see Figure 7.1).

② Double-click the icon to the left of A-Master A. Master A will then be displayed. A broken Chain icon at the top left of a page indicates the page is a master page.

✦ In the case of Facing Page documents, Master A comprises both left and right-hand pages.

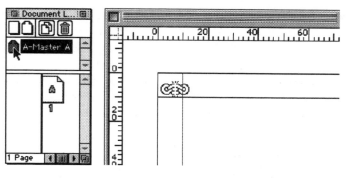

Figure 7.1 Master page icon in the Document Layout palette (left) and
'chain' icon at the top left hand corner of a master page (right)

Adding headers and footers within Master A

① Create text boxes in the top and bottom margin areas (on
both left and right-hand pages in the case of a Facing Pages
document).

② Enter text and format in the usual way.

Closing Master A

Either:

• choose Document from the Display sub-menu in the Page
menu.

Or:

• double-click any document page in the Document Layout
palette.

▲ Because master page items appear on all pages of your document, ensure
they are accurately placed and formatted. Provided you do not alter the
items locally on individual document pages, you can always return to the
items on Master A and make alterations and these alterations will be
reproduced on all document pages.

You can re-apply master page items to individual document pages, by click-
dragging the A-Master A icon over a document page icon in the Document
Layout palette. Altered items on a page will be kept or deleted depending
on the setting in the Master Page Items pop-up menu in the General set of
controls in the Document Preferences for... dialog box.

Page numbering

Managing page numbers

By default, page numbers in QuarkXPress follow the order of
the pages in the Document Layout palette. Thus the third page
of the document will be labelled Page 3 at the bottom of the
document window and Document Layout palette and numbered
3 on the document page itself (should a page number code be
present).

You can alter the page numbering at any time to meet your editorial needs. Page numbering sequences (called Sections in
QuarkXPress) can start on any document page. Bear in mind
however that section start numbers must be even on left-hand
pages and odd on right-hand pages in Facing Pages documents.
Otherwise the first page in a section will automatically be
moved to the correct side of the document's spine.

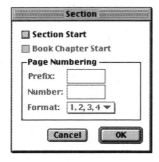

Figure 7.2 The Section dialog box

Each section can have a different numbering format from a
choice of Roman and Arabic characters.

Sections and their page numbering sequences are respected
when documents are linked together (see *Linking documents*,
page 90). If chapters (linked documents) lack sections, page
numbers continue from the previous chapter. In other words,
whether sections are present or not within chapters, the numbering regime within a book corresponds to the numbering
regime within a single document.

Page numbers only appear on pages if the page number code <#> is present. The code may be entered within a text box either on a master page or directly on a document page. If you do not wish a number to be present, as might be the case for a chapter start, delete the code or remove the text box on the document page.

Adding page numbers within Master A

① Open A-Master A as shown previously.

② Create text boxes in the top, bottom or side margin areas (on both left and right-hand pages in the case of a Facing Pages document).

③ Within the text box(s) press ⌘ + #3. The page number code <#> will appear. Format the code as you would format normal text.

In Windows use the Control key instead of the Command key.

④ Double-click on any document page icon on the Document Layout palette to return to the document pages. The page number will be present and correct for each page.

Restarting page number sequences

① Choose Document Layout from the View menu. The Document Layout palette will be displayed (see Figure 7.3).

② Double-click the page at which you wish the page numbering to restart.

Figure 7.3 Specifying a section start

③ Choose Section... from the Page menu. The Section dialog box will be displayed.

④ Check or tick Section Start.

⑤ Enter a number in the Number field or leave it as 1.

⑥ Choose a style of Arabic or Roman numbering in the Format pop-up menu.

⑦ Click OK. An asterisk will appear after the page number in the document window and Document Layout palette indicating a section start.

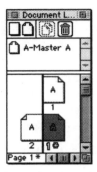

Figure 7.4 An asterisk beside a page number indicates a section start

Adding other master pages

Creating additional master pages

① Choose Document Layout from the View menu. The Document Layout palette will be displayed (see Figure 7.5).

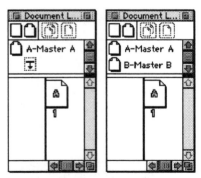

Figure 7.5 Create a master page by click-dragging a blank page icon into the upper window of the Document Layout palette

② Click-drag the Blank Facing Pages icon (second icon, top row) to within the same window as Master A. (In the case of a non-facing pages document, use the Blank Single Page icon.)

③ Double-click the new icon to the left of Master B. Master B will then be displayed. A broken Chain icon at the top left of a page indicates the page is a master page.

④ Choose Master Guides... from the Page menu. The Master Guides dialog box will be displayed (see Figure 7.6).

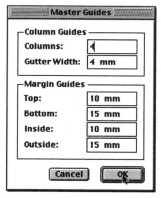

Figure 7.6 Amending column guides

⑤ Enter new values in the Column Guides and Margin Guides fields, as required.

⑥ Click OK.

⑦ Choose Document from the Display sub-menu in the Page menu.

Creating linked master pages

Use this technique to automatically link text boxes across pages. Once linked, new pages will automatically be created as text boxes overfill.

Where new pages are added in a document depends on the current setting in the Auto Page Insertion pop-up menu in the General set of controls in the Document preferences for... dialog box.

Adding text boxes to a master page

① Create and open a new master page.

② Add text boxes to the master page(s) in the usual way.

Linking the text boxes to the pages

① Hold down [Alt] and select the Linking tool in the Tools palette. Release [Alt] and the mouse button.

② Move the pointer over the broken chain icon at the top left of the page and click once, move the pointer over the first text box on the page and click once again, move the pointer over the second text box and click once again and so on.

③ Turn off the Linking tool by selecting the Item or Content tool.

④ Repeat for the right-hand page if you are working in a facing pages document.

⑤ Close the master page.

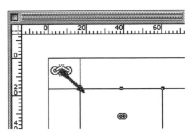

Figure 7.7 Linking a text box to a master page

Linking documents

For flexibility, you may wish to divide a large publication into separate documents. This will allow more than one person to work on a publication at the same time and enable you to work with smaller files.

Documents used this way are called chapters and a collection of linked documents is called a book. You control chapters using the Book palette which automatically synchronizes style sheets and manages page numbering sequences.

Creating a book

Creating a new book

① Choose Book from the New sub-menu in the File menu. The New Book directory dialog box will be displayed (see Figure 7.8).

② Enter a name in the Book Name field.

③ Select a drive and folder in which to save the file.

④ Click Create. The Book palette will be displayed.

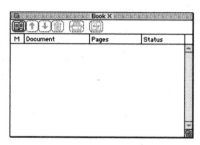

Figure 7.8 A newly created book palette

Opening a book

① Choose Open... from the File menu. The Open directory dialog box will be displayed (see Figure 7.9).

② Use the directory dialog box controls to locate your book.

③ Click Open. The Book palette will be displayed.

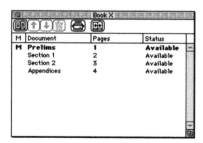

Figure 7.9 A book palette listing four chapters

Adding chapters to a book

① Click the Add icon in the Book palette (see Figure 7.10).

② Use the directory dialog box controls to locate the document you wish to add.

③ Click Add. The document will be added to the Book palette as the first chapter.

④ Repeat steps 1–3 to add other documents as chapters.

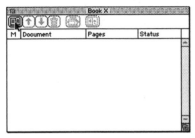

Figure 7.10 Adding a chapter to the book palette

Checking the status of chapters

• Look at the status column for each chapter. The status will be Available, Open, 'User Name', Modified or Missing.

If the status of any chapter is Missing, double-click the chapter name. The Find "..." directory dialog box will be displayed. Locate and select the missing chapter file using the directory dialog box controls. Click Open.

If the status of any chapter is Modified, open the chapter file resave it and close it.

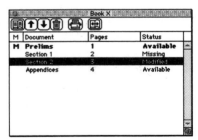

Figure 7.11 Updating a chapter in a book

✦ Available status means the chapter file can be opened. Open status means
the chapter file is already open on your computer. 'User Name' status
means the chapter file is open on another person's computer. Modified
status means the chapter file has been opened and modified from outside
the Book palette controls. Missing status means the chapter file is no longer
linked to the Book palette. This is usually because the file has since been
moved or renamed.

Creating a table of contents

Style sheets can be used as a basis for generating tables of contents for long documents and books.

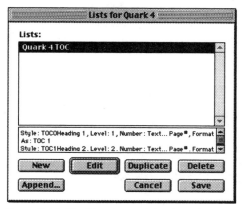

Figure 7.12 The Lists for... dialog box

① Choose Lists... from the Edit menu. The Lists for... dialog box will be displayed.

② Click New. The Edit List dialog box will be displayed (see Figure 7.12).

③ Enter a name in the Name field.

Adding style sheets to a table of contents list

① Double-click a style sheet name in the Available Styles window. The style sheet will automatically be entered into the Styles List window.

② Repeat the previous step a number of times until you have added all the style sheets you need for the table of contents.

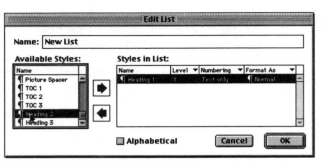

Figure 7.13 Including a style sheet in a list

Removing style sheets from a table of contents list

① Select the style sheet name in the Styles in List window.

② Click the left-pointing arrow.

Assigning attributes to each 'table of contents' item

① Select the first style sheet in the Styles in List window.

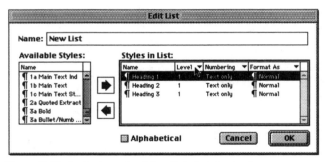

Figure 7.14 Assigning a level to a listed style sheet

② Choose an option in the Level pop-up menu; 1 will give the top level, 2 will give the next level and so on.

③ Choose either Text...Page* or Page*...Text in the Numbering pop-up menu.

④ Choose one of your table of contents style sheets from the Format As pop-up menu. If you have not already created style sheets for your table of contents, leave the setting as you find it and return to this menu after you have done so.

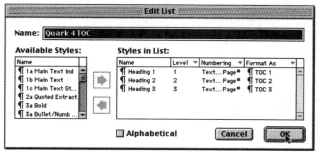

Figure 7.15 A completed list

Generating a table of contents

① Choose Show Lists from the View menu. The Lists palette will be displayed.

② Choose Current Document from the Show List pop-up menu. The Lists palette will be displayed (see Figure 7.16).

③ Click Update to make sure the table of contents will take into account any modifications you might have made to the Edit Lists dialog box.

Figure 7.16 Updating the Lists palette

④ Select the text box in which you wish to generate the table of contents.

⑤ Click Build to generate the table.

Figure 7.17 Building a table of contents

Updating an existing table of contents setting

① Choose Show Lists from the View menu. The Lists palette will be displayed.

② Choose Current Document from the Show List pop-up menu. The Lists palette will be displayed (see Figure 7.17).

③ Click Update to make sure the table of contents will take into account any modifications you might have made to the Edit Lists dialog box.

④ Remove the existing table of contents setting and keep the text box selected.

⑤ Click Build to generate an up-to-date table of contents.

Making an index

Enabling the index XTension

① Choose XTensions Manager... from the Utilities menu.

② Select Index and click to left of name. A tick indicates it's enabled.

③ Click OK.

④ Close all documents, quit QuarkXPress and reload the program.

Create character style sheets for index entries

Creating one level index entries

① Choose Index from the View menu. The Index palette will be displayed.

In this palette, you can add words at one of four index levels, determine the scope of index references, create cross-references and edit and delete entries. Here we will just create a first-level index entry.

Figure 7.18 Creating an index entry

② Select a word or words in your document which you wish to include in the index. The word(s) appears in the Text field in the Index palette.

③ If you wish the word(s) to read differently in the index, edit the text in the field whilst it is still selected on the page.

④ Choose First Level from the Level pop-up menu.

⑤ Choose a character style sheet from the Style pop-up menu if you wish the page numbers to differ from the text. This step is optional.

⑥ Choose Selection Start from the Scope pop-up menu if you wish the page number to refer to the start of the selection or choose Selection Text when a selection runs from page to page and you wish the index to refer to more than one page.

⑦ Click Add (see Figure 7.18). A square [bracket] around the selected text shows that it is an index entry.

Creating two-level index entries

① Choose Index from the View menu. The Index palette will be displayed.

② Select a word or words in your document which you wish to include in the index at a first level.

Figure 7.19 Creating a second-level entry

③ Choose First Level from the Level pop-up menu.

④ Choose Suppress page* from the Scope pop-up menu.

⑤ Click Add (see Figure 7.19). A square [bracket] around the selected text shows that it is an index entry.

⑥ Select a word or words in your document which you wish to include in the index at a second level.

⑦ Choose Second Level from the Level pop-up menu.

⑧ Choose Selection Start from the Scope pop-up menu if you wish the page number to refer to the start of the selection or choose Selection Text when a selection runs from page to page more and you wish the index to refer to more than one page.

⑨ Click to the left of the first level entry under which you wish to list the entry. The small arrow will move beside the entry.

⑩ Click Add. A square [bracket] around the selected text shows that it is an index entry.

Editing index entries

① Select an entry in the entries list.

② Click the Edit button (pencil icon) or double-click the entry name. The pencil icon turns black to indicate that it is enabled.

③ Make any changes in the Text or Sort As fields.

④ Click the Edit button (pencil icon) again or click another entry name. The pencil icon turns white to indicate that it is disabled.

Deleting index entries

① Select an entry in the entries list.

② Click the Delete.

Building indexes

Before you can build any index you need first to create a special
master page with linked text boxes. See *Creating linked master
pages* (page 89).

If you wish to format index text automatically you also need to
prepare suitable style sheets in advance, especially if you are
compiling a multi-level index.

Building an index

① With the Content tool active, select the first text box on the
first index page. This page must be based on a linked master
page.

② Choose Build Index... from the Utilities menu. The Build
Index dialog box will be displayed (see Figure 7.20).

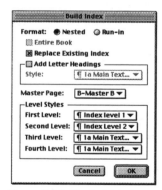

Figure 7.20 The Build Index dialog box

③ If you just wish to index an open chapter (a linked
document), uncheck or untick Entire Book. Otherwise leave
checked or ticked. The checkbox will be dimmed in
independent documents.

④ Check or tick Replace Index if you wish to replace an existing
index. Otherwise leave unchecked or unticked.

⑤ Check or tick Add Letter Headings if you wish letters to proceed each set of alphabetical entries. In this case, choose a style sheet from the Style pop-up menu. Otherwise leave unchecked or unticked.

⑥ Choose an Automatic Text Box master page from the Master Page pop-up menu.

⑦ Choose style sheets for the index from the Level Styles pop-up menus.

⑧ Click OK. The index will flow into the linked boxes.

Summary

- **Headers and footers** Repeated items, such as headers, footers, page numbers and logos, can be placed on master pages for automatic inclusion on document pages.

- **Adding page numbers** A special page number code provides the correct page number for each document page.

- **Altering page numbers** Documents can contain different page numbering sequences.

- **Compiling a table of contents** Content tables can be generated automatically by linking style sheets within the Edit List dialog box.

- **Linking documents** Large publications can be worked on as separate documents and linked together as chapters using the Book palette.

- **Compiling an index** Indexes can be generated automatically after locally assigning text within a document.

08

working with items

In this chapter you will learn:
- how to select and manipulate items
- how to draw lines and boxes
- how to frame and transform items

Selecting and manipulating items

Items – text boxes, picture boxes and lines – are normally selected with the Item tool and item attributes are applied through the Item menu. You can use the Content tool to select and alter the dimensions of individual items.

The Item tool must be active, however, if you wish to move or copy items using the clipboard, otherwise an item's content will be moved or copied instead of the item itself.

The Item tool must also be active if more than one item is to be selected.

Selecting and deselecting items

Selecting multiple items

① With the Item tool active, click on the first item.

② Hold down ⌈Shift⌉ and click on other items to be selected.

▲ Clicking an item a second time when the Shift key is held down will deselect an item, a third time reselect an item and so on.

Selecting multiple items by marqueeing

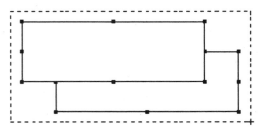

Figure 8.1 Marqueeing two boxes

• With the Item tool active, click-drag from a point on the blank area of the page diagonally across all the items to be selected.

Selecting all items on a spread

- With the Item tool active, choose Select All from the Edit menu.

Deselecting all items on a spread

Either:

- click a blank part of a page.

Or:

- with the Item tool active, press [Tab].

Selecting underlying items

① With the Item tool or Content tool active, hold down [⌘][Alt][Shift] and click on the overlaying item.

In Windows use the Control key instead of the Command key.

② Click once more to select the item immediately underneath.

③ Click once again to select a further underlaying item and so on.

④ Release all keys.

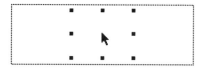

Figure 8.2 Selecting an underlaying item

Positioning and sizing items using guides

You can snap the edges or ends of items to column and margin guides for accurate positioning and sizing. The snap distance is governed by the setting in the General set of controls in the Document Preferences for... dialog box. If you wish to locate an item, such as a line, close to a guide without the cursor being attracted to it, just temporarily disable the function.

- Choose Snap to Guides from the View menu to enable/disable the function. A tick indicates that it's selected.

Positioning items on the pasteboard

You can place items on pasteboards as well as on pages. You may, for instance, wish to import a large amount of text which you plan to subsequently split into different stories. It makes sense to import the text into a box positioned away from page areas so it doesn't disturb any page layout content. Sometimes you may wish to move an item temporarily away from a page to make it easier to access other items or just to see how the layout looks without it. The pasteboard is an ideal place to park such items.

Positioning and sizing items using coordinates

① With the Item tool active, select an item or items.

② Enter values – millimetres or points – in the X, Y, W and H fields in the Measurements palette. Press [Enter ↵].

Locking items in position

Very small or large items can be locked to a page so they cannot be moved accidentally through the use of the mouse.

① With the Item tool active, select an item or items.

② Choose Lock from the Item menu. A padlock icon will appear if you try to move or resize the item.

Fig. 8.3 A padlock icon indicates that an item is locked

✦ Locked items can be moved by the cursor keys only and are *not* protected from accidental deletion.

Duplicating items

① With the Item tool active, select an item or items.

② Choose Duplicate from the Item menu. The duplicate will be offset from the original item(s).

Grouping items together

Related items, such as logos and slogans, can be grouped so that they act as a single entity while the Item tool is selected.

Grouping items

① With the Item tool active, select the items you wish to group.

② Choose Group from the Item menu. A dotted border will appear when a group is selected with the Item tool.

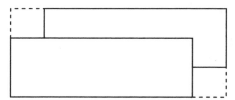

Figure 8.4 A dashed bounding box indicates that items are grouped

✦ You can modify items within a group with the Content tool active.

Moving items in front of/behind each other

All items, including text and picture boxes, have a stacking order. Older items always underlap newer items when you position them together. You can alter the stacking order at any time for either access or layout purposes.

Changing the stacking order of items

① With either the Item tool or Content tool active, select the item to be moved.

② Choose Send to Back or Bring to Front from the Item menu.

▲ Hold down the Alt key when you pull down the Item menu for the additional commands Send Backward and Bring Forward.

Moving and copying items using the clipboard

Items are either moved or copied from page to page or from document to document using the clipboard (a short-term storage area assigned for this purpose). Any item which you cut or copy is automatically placed on the clipboard.

However many times you paste, the item will remain on the clipboard until another item is cut or copied.

▲ The current contents of the clipboard can be viewed at any time by choosing View clipboard from the Edit menu.

Moving items elsewhere

① With the Item tool active, select the item or items you wish to move, by using one of the methods described previously. Choose Cut from the Edit menu.

② Move to the page where you wish to move the item and choose Paste from the Edit menu. The item will be pasted in the centre of the document window.

Copying items elsewhere

① With the Item tool active, select the item or items you wish to copy. Choose Copy from the Edit menu.

② Move to the page where you wish to place the item and choose Paste from the Edit menu. The item will be pasted in the centre of the document window.

Anchored text and picture boxes

Sometimes you may wish to include a text or picture box within a text area and have it move with the text during editing work. The way you achieve this is to 'anchor' a box within the text. The process is essentially quite simple and makes use of the clipboard.

Usually, when the clipboard is used, *either* the Content *or* Item tool is active throughout the cutting/copying and pasting process. In the case of anchored items, the *Item tool* is active when the item is cut or copied. The *Content tool* is active for the pasting stage. It's an ingenious use of the clipboard.

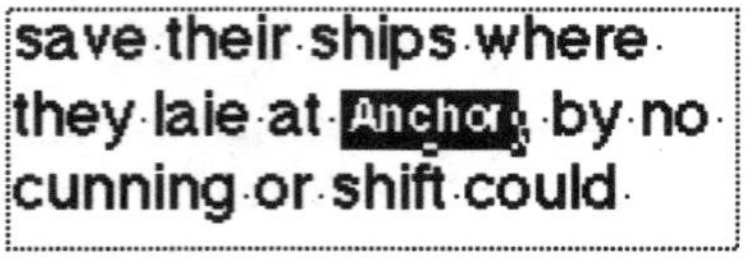

```
save their ships where
they laie at Anchor by no
cunning or shift could
```

Figure 8.5 A small text box anchored within a paragraph

Anchoring a box in text

① Create a text box in the usual way, but make its height no larger than the leading of the text in which it is going to be anchored (to match the example shown).

② Insert text into the box and then format it.

③ Select the Item tool.

④ Choose Cut or Copy from the Edit menu.

⑤ Select the Content tool.

⑥ In another text box, position the insertion point where you wish to anchor the new box within the text.

⑦ Choose Paste from the Edit menu. A three-handled text box will be anchored in the text.

▲ Use the same process to anchor picture boxes in text.

Moving an anchored box relative to the text baseline

① With either the Content tool or Item tool active, select the anchored text box.

② Select either alignment option at the far left of the Measurements palette.

③ In addition or alternatively, with either the Content tool or Item tool active, select the area underlying the anchored box as you would select normal text and choose Baseline Shift... from the Style menu. Enter a positive or negative value.

④ Click OK.

Adding lines and arrows

Use vertical lines (rules) to separate columns of text and horizontal lines to separate articles. Diagonal lines give layouts a dynamic quality and curved and wavy lines can add further visual interest. Lines can be used, with or without arrows, to link captions to pictures.

① Select either the orthogonal or diagonal line tool by clicking once only on its icon in the Tool palette.

② Move the mouse (without pressing the button) over the page. The pointer turns into a cross hair. Move the cross hair to where you wish one end of the line to be.

③ Click-drag (press the mouse button and move the mouse with the button depressed) to where you wish the other end of the line to be. Release the mouse button.

④ Choose attributes from the sub-menus in the Style menu.

Figure 8.6 Creating a rule and adding an arrow

▲ Hold down the Shift key to constrain a diagonal line to 45° increments.

See section *Drawing lines and boxes* (below) for how to create loosely drawn and curved lines.

Drawing lines and boxes

Drawing bézier lines, text paths and boxes

Lines and shapes can be drawn loosely using the freehand tool variants or accurately using the bézier tools variants. Either way, items are constructed out of path segments connected by anchor points. The advantage of this system is that it's completely editable. Anchor points can be moved and deleted and curves altered at any time until the right effect is achieved.

Text can be attached to lines (called paths) and flowed with shaped boxes to created interesting text effects.

Variants of the tools work in the same way, so once you have mastered the picture box bézier tool, for instance, you will have mastered all the other bézier tools in the toolbox.

Drawing loosely

① Select one of the freehand bézier tool variants by clicking once only on its icon in the Tool palette.

② Move the mouse (without pressing the button) over the page. The pointer turns into a cross hair. Move the cross hair to where you wish to begin a line or the outline of a shape.

③ Click-drag (press the mouse button and move the mouse with the button depressed) to draw a line or outline. Release the mouse button. The completed path will be defined by a series of anchor points with intervening segments.

Either:

④ Choose attributes from the sub-menus in the Style menu, if you have used the freehand bézier line tool.

Or:

④ With the Content tool active, type in text using the keyboard, if you have used the freehand bézier text box tool.

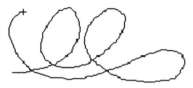

Figure 8.7 A linear flourish created using the freehand bézier line tool

Drawing accurately

① Select one of the bézier tool variants by clicking once only on its icon in the Tool palette.

② Move the mouse (without pressing the button) over the page. The pointer turns into a cross hair. Move the cross hair to where you wish to begin a line or the outline of a shape.

③ Click or click-drag a number of times to draw a line or outline (see Figure 8.8).

If you are using a bézier box tool you will need to finally close the path. To do so:

④ Either: click on the first anchor point you created.

A rounded-corner box icon will appear as you move the bézier tool towards the point. If this icon does not appear, then you are trying to connect to the wrong point.

Or: double-click the last-but-one anchor point.

Either way the completed path will be defined by a series of anchor points with intervening segments.

If you have used the freehand bézier text box tool you will need to add text to the path. To do so:

⑤ with the Content tool active, type in text using the keyboard. Once entered, text can be edited and formatted in the normal manner.

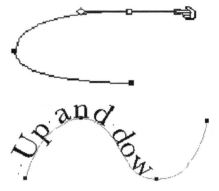

Figure 8.8 Drawing a path with a bézier tool (top); text following the path (bottom)

Mastering the bézier tools

Create a path by clicking or click-dragging with the bézier tool. Clicking the bézier tool creates a straight line segment that ends in a corner anchor point; click-dragging the bézier tool creates a curved segment with an associated smooth anchor point, complete with direction handles.

As you click-drag to create a curved segment, adjust the length and angle of the leading direction handle (the one which the pen tool is controlling) to create a trailing segment of the right curvature.

The bézier tools work in the similar way as their counterparts in Adobe Illustrator, Macromedia FreeHand and Adobe Photoshop. If you have not used the pen tool in any of these programs, you might find the following toy boat analogy useful when drawing curved segments.

Imagine when you draw curves that you are pulling a toy boat along in a pond. As you click-drag, it's as though you are pulling a string attached to the boat. As you 'pull', a curved segment is formed, like the wake of a boat. By altering the length and angle of the 'string', the curve of the 'wake' is altered. When you are happy with the curve, release the 'string'.

When drawing paths bear the following in mind.

- Create only as many anchor points as you need to draw a path, especially in the case of smooth points. The adage 'Less is more' can be adopted as a good rule-of-thumb when drawing bézier paths.

- Position smooth anchor points either where curves change direction (where a left-hand curve changes into a right-hand curve) or at the tops and bottoms of curves. Do so by click-dragging from these positions.

- Avoid creating anchor points over ends of direction lines (the handles which show when a point is selected), as it leads to confusion.

Altering bézier paths

Moving an anchor point

① With either the Content tool or Item tool active, select the item.

② Click-drag the point.

Adjusting a curve segment

① With either the Content tool or Item tool active, select the item.

② Either:

click-drag the curve segment.

Or:

② click on a point. A triangular icon will indicate that the point is selected.

③ Click-drag the end of the direction line.

Merging and reshaping items

Merging items

Items can be merged in a number of ways within QuarkXPress.

① With the Item tool active, select the items you wish to merge.

② Choose an option from the Merge sub-menu in the Item menu.

Merging effects

Intersection creates a single item where multiple items overlap.

Union creates a single item out of multiple items.

Difference subtracts overlaying items from an underlying item.

Reverse Difference subtracts an underlaying item from overlaying items.

Exclusive Or and *Combine* both create a single item out of multiple items with an aperture where items overlapped.

Reshaping boxes

Switching between standard box shapes

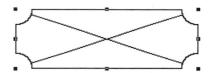

Figure 8.9 Box created by concave-corner picture box tool

① With either the Content tool or Item tool active, select a text or picture box.

② Select an option in the Box Shape sub-menu in the Item menu.

Spacing and aligning items

You can accurately space and align items using the Space/Align controls. The controls are not particularly intuitive; experiment with items until you fully understand the effects of each pop-up menu and radio button option.

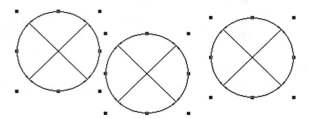

Figure 8.10 Selected items ready for alignment

Figure 8.11 Items vertically aligned and horizontally distributed

① With the Item tool active, select more than one item.

② Choose Space/Align... from the Item menu. The Space/Align Items dialog box will be displayed (see Figure 8.12).

③ Check or tick the Horizontal box to set horizontal spacing and alignments.

④ Check or tick the Vertical box to set vertical spacing and alignments.

⑤ Click OK.

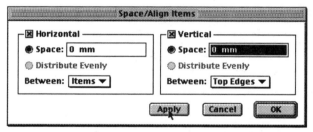

Figure 8.12 The Space/Align dialog box

Framing and transforming items

Framing text and picture boxes

Text and picture boxes can be given printed borders for emphasis and for defining areas. These borders (or box rules) are called Frames.

Framing text and picture boxes

① With either the Item tool or Content tool active, select a text or picture box.

② Choose Frame... from the Item menu. The Frame set of controls will be displayed (see Figure 8.13).

③ Choose a frame in the Style window and enter a value, other than 0, in the Width field. Select a Colour and/or Shade attribute as required.

④ Click OK.

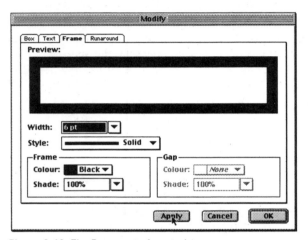

Figure 8.13 The Frame set of controls

▲ Large picture boxes can be placed on pages and framed to give a printed border (box rule). It can be a wise precaution to lock boxes used for this purpose and bring guides to the front so they are showing. If you've made the box after other items, you will need, of course, to send the box to the back so that the other items are in front.

Rotating text and picture boxes

You can rotate text and pictures to give either vertical or diagonal emphasis to a page layout.

Rotating a text or picture box by specifying an angle

① With either the Item tool or Content tool active, select a text or picture box.

② Enter a value in the Box Angle field in the Measurements palette. Press [Enter ↵].

! When specifying rotation angles for large items or items positioned near the edge of a page, it is necessary to allow for sufficient rotation space. Move an item into the centre of the page first, rotate the item and then reposition it.

+ Items rotated by entering a value are rotated about the item's centre-point.

Rotating a text or picture box using the Rotation tool

① With either the Item tool or Content tool active, select a text or picture box.

② Select the Rotation tool in the Tool palette and click at the point of rotation and, without releasing the mouse button, drag away from the point to create a 'lever'; follow it with a movement in a clockwise or anti-clockwise direction.

③ Release the mouse button.

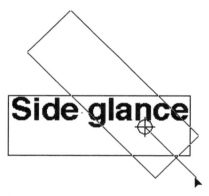

Figure 8.14 Rotating a box using the Rotate tool

! Rotating and skewing images within a QuarkXPress document substantially increases printing and imagesetting times and can prevent a document from outputting at all. This is because the remapping of the image is implemented during the outputting process and it is demanding on processing time. To avoid this problem rotate or skew images in the source documents.

▲ Hold down the Shift key when using the Rotation tool to rotate in 45° increments.

Skewing text and images

You can skew text and images for visual effect.

① With either the Item tool or Content tool active, select a text or picture box.

② Choose Modify... from the Item menu. The Box or Text set of controls will be displayed.

③ Enter a value in the Skew or Text Skew field.

④ Click OK.

Flipping text and picture boxes

You can flip text and images horizontally and/or vertically for special effect.

Figure 8.15 Rotating a box using the Rotate tool

① With either the Item tool or Content tool active, select a text or picture box.

Either:

② choose Flip Horizontal or Vertical from the Style menu.

Or:

② click on the Horizontal or Vertical arrow icons in the middle of the Measurements palette.

Summary

- **Item tool** Use the Item tool for multiple selections or for moving items with or without the clipboard.

- **Creating borders** Boxes can be used to create borders or simple graphic elements.

- **Keeping items in place** Lock items which are small or very large so they can't be moved accidentally.

- **Keeping items together** Group items together if their spatial relationship needs to be maintained.

- **Working within groups** Use the Content tool for selecting and manipulating text, images and boxes within groups.

- **Drawing in QuarkXPress** The freehand and bézier tool variants enable you to create curved lines and shapes without resorting to a separate draw program.

- **Running text along and inside paths** Text can run along paths or fill shapes created by one of the text path and text box creation tools.

09 importing images

In this chapter you will learn:
- how to work with picture boxes
- ways of working with images
- about different file formats
- how to store images

Working with picture boxes

Picture boxes within QuarkXPress are the equivalent to the pasted-down photographs or drawn picture rectangles used in conventional artwork. You place images in these boxes which you create on document pages as you work.

The standard picture box is rectangular. You can create other shaped boxes including rounded-corner, concave-corner, bevelled-corner and oval. You can also draw boxes to your own shape using the freehand and bézier picture box tools.

Picture boxes define the crop (visible area) of images; their size and position together with text boxes, determines the page layout.

They are also used without graphics to create coloured panels and borders (box rules) in which case they can be specified as having no content (this optional setting removes the cross lines identifying picture boxes when guides are showing).

Picture boxes are often aligned with margin, column or ruler guides for accurate positioning.

You can place as many picture boxes as you like on a document page. They can always be altered in size and the images within them changed.

Creating and resizing picture boxes

Creating a picture box

① Select the Rectangular Picture Box tool by clicking once only on its icon in the Tool palette.

② Move the mouse (without pressing the button) over the page. The pointer turns into a cross hair. Move the cross hair to where you wish the top left of the box to be (marked A in Figure 9.1).

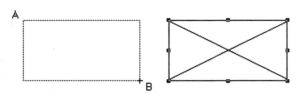

Figure 9.1 Creating a picture box

③ Click-drag (press the mouse button and move the mouse with the button depressed) diagonally to where you wish the bottom right corner of the box to be (marked B in Figure 9.1). Release the mouse button.

▲ You can use the same process to create other standard box shapes. See Chapter 8, *Working with items* for how to use the freehand and bézier picture box tools.

Resizing a picture box

① With either the Item tool or Content tool active, click once somewhere within a box (if not already selected). Move the pointer to one of the handles at the bottom of the picture box. The pointer turns into a pointing hand.

② Whilst the pointing hand is displayed, click-drag the handle downwards to resize the box.

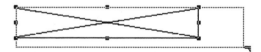

Figure 9.2 Resizing a picture box

▲ Handles halfway along the side of boxes can be used to enlarge or reduce a box in one dimension only. Corner handles enable you to enlarge or reduce both dimensions of a box in one operation.

Moving and deleting picture boxes

Moving a picture box or other item

• With the Item tool active, click-drag the middle of an item.

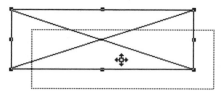

Figure 9.3 Moving a picture box

▲ To move an item whilst the Content tool is selected, hold down the Command key whilst click-dragging the item.

Deleting a picture box or other item

Either:

• with the Item tool active, press [Delete] (back space).

Or:

• with either the Item tool or Content tool active, choose Delete from the Item menu.

Ways of working with images

You can't create images apart from simple vector drawings within QuarkXPress since it's primarily a page layout program. You create bitmapped images within specialized paint programs or by scanning photographs and more complex vector images for illustrations and charts within specialized draw, chart and spreadsheet programs.

Vector images are comprised of mathematically-described PostScript paths either drawn by users on-screen or created automatically by programs. The images are resolution-free and scalable, which makes the technology ideal for logotypes, charts and other visual devices, the sizes of which cannot be pre-determined. Bitmapped images are mosaics of pixels, often created by scanning originals, such as photographs, and invariably manipulated by users on-screen. They have a resolution (usually measured in pixels per inch) which limits how much they can be rescaled.

Scanned (bitmapped) images, unlike vector images, have large file sizes which can create storage problems. Additionally, good scanning equipment is expensive and scanning is an art in itself. However, there are several strategies you can adopt if you lack sufficient storage capacity or the appropriate equipment and/or expertise. One way is to import roughly scanned, low resolution, images into your documents. These images will be good enough to work with and may be good enough to print from, and will give an indication of the treatment and positioning of images to all concerned.

After you have completed your documents, professionally scanned, high resolution versions of images can be substituted for the low resolution images, whether you are planning to imageset your documents or just wish to have the best possible printing quality. The advantage of this approach is that you avoid having to store large picture files on your system and you leave the accurate scanning work to others. This basic idea has been incorporated into a system called OPI, a sophisticated process of image duplication and file substitution used for the imagesetting of large documents involving many images.

Another way is to import accurately scanned images from the start. If you have neither the skills nor the equipment to produce scans to the right quality, ask your bureau to carry out this work before you start the page layout process.

A final way is simply not to worry about scanning at all at the page layout stage; just create picture boxes and frame them. The printed frames indicate where the images will go and you supply your bureau with the original transparencies and prints and tell them which image goes where and how they are to be sized and cropped.

If you are working with vectored drawings and charts, no scanning is involved so any imported drawings and charts should print well, provided you have saved them in the appropriate file format.

Inserting images

When you import, as opposed to paste, scanned and vectored images into a QuarkXPress document, low resolution bitmapped versions of the original images are placed within the document for layout purposes (unless files are in PICT format, in which case the images are embedded at full resolution). Links between the placement images and their originals are automatically made during the importing process.

When you output your documents, QuarkXPress takes the data detailing the position, scaling and cropping of the placement images and applies it to the original images which it uses for outputting purposes.

You can insert images into picture boxes in many ways. One method is covered here. The use of the clipboard method is explained later in this chapter.

✦ The tonal/colour quality of embedded bitmapped images is set within the Application Preferences dialog box. Set at the lowest quality if you wish to keep your QuarkXPress file sizes as small as possible.

Importing images using Get Picture

① With the Content tool active, select a picture box.

② Choose Get Picture... from the File menu. The Get Picture directory dialog box will be displayed.

③ Use the directory dialog box controls to locate the picture.

④ Click Open.

Selecting images

An image is selected by clicking once on its picture box with the Content tool active.

The pointer turns into a grabber hand on the selected image.

Figure 9.4 The content tool cursor changes into a grabber hand when selecting images

Deleting images

• With the Content tool active, select the picture box and press [Delete] (back space).

Cropping, scaling and fitting images

Cropping pictures

① With the Content tool active, select an image.

Either:

② click-drag the image within the picture box.

Figure 9.5 Moving an image within a picture box using the Content tool

Or:

② press ⬅, ➡, ⬇ or ⬆ to move the image in 1pt increments.

Or:

② enter values in the X+ (pt or mm across) and Y+ (pt or mm vertically) fields in the Measurements palette.

Or:

② resize the picture box.

▲ When using the Arrow keys, hold down the Alt key to move in 0.1pt increments.

Scaling images

① With the Content tool active, select an image.

Either:

② enter values in the X% (% width) and Y% (% height) fields in the Measurements palette.

Figure 9.6 Scaling box and image together using the cursor in conjunction with selected keystokes

Or:

② press `⌘` `Alt` `Shift` + `>.` to increase the scale in 5% increments. Use `<,` to decrease the scale.

In Windows use the Control key instead of the Command key.

Or:

② hold down `⌘` `Alt` `Shift` and click-drag a corner handle of the picture box.

In Windows use the Control key instead of the Command key.

❗ Avoid enlarging images more than 165%, as image degradation may take place when outputting.

Centring images within picture boxes

- With the Content tool active, select an image and press `⌘` `Shift` + `M` (for Middle) and click a corner handle of the picture box.

In Windows use the Control key instead of the Command key.

Fitting images within picture boxes without distortion

- With the Content tool active, select an image and press down `⌘` `Alt` `Shift` + `F` (for Fit).

In Windows use the Control key instead of the Command key.

Fitting images within picture boxes

This technique inevitably results in image distortion unless the proportions of a picture box exactly matches the proportions of the image.

- With the Content tool active, select the picture box and press down [⌘] [Shift] + [F] (for Fit).

  In Windows use the Control key instead of the Command key.

! Using distorted images within a QuarkXPress document substantially increases printing and imagesetting times and can prevent a document from outputting at all. To avoid this problem either distort images in source documents or maintain the proportions of images.

Moving and copying images using the clipboard

Moving and copying images is normally done using the clipboard. Any images which you cut or copy are automatically placed on the clipboard.

However many times you paste, an image will remain on the clipboard until other content is cut or copied.

Moving images

① With the Content tool active, select the image you wish to move. Choose Cut from the Edit menu.

② Select the picture box to which you wish to move the image and choose Paste from the Edit menu.

Copying images

① With the Content tool active, select the image you wish to copy. Choose Copy from the Edit menu.

② Select the picture box to which you wish to place the copied image and choose Paste from the Edit menu.

Colouring, shading and inverting images

Line and grayscale images can be coloured and inverted (made negative) for visual effect. Line images can also be shaded.

Colouring images

① With the Content tool active, select the picture box.

② Choose an option from the colour and Shade sub-menus in the Style menu.

Figure 9.7 Logo (left) made negative (right)

Inverting images

① With the Content tool active, select the picture box.

② Choose Negative from the Style menu.

Skewing picture boxes and images

Figure 9.8 A image skewed in a picture box

Images can be skewed within a QuarkXPress document for visual effect. This can be achieved by skewing a picture box (which effectively skews any image within it as well), by skewing the image itself (independently of the box it's within as well) or by skewing an image before importation, using an image manipulation program, such as Adobe Photoshop.

Skewing images

① With the Content tool active, select a picture box.

Either:

② choose Modify... from the Item menu.

③ click the Box tab.

④ Enter a value in the Box Skew field to skew a box together with its contents.

⑤ Click OK.

Or:

② enter a value in the Skew field in the Measurements palette to skew an image independently of its box.

Running text around images

Text can run around picture boxes or the profile of images within boxes. Normally when a picture box is placed above a text box, text in the underlying box is displaced. The control which causes this effect is called Runaround.

 Without further ado the spotted dog was heading back home for his dinner.

Figure 9.9 Text running around the edges of a picture box

Adjusting the runaround distance

① With either the Item tool or Content tool active, select the overlying picture box.

② Choose Runaround... from the Item menu. The Runaround set of controls will be displayed (see Figure 9.10).

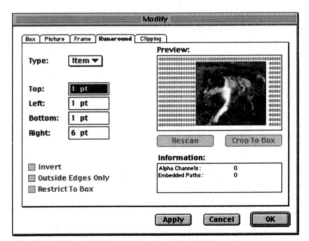

Figure 9.10 Specifying text to runaround the edges of a picture box

③ Choose Item from the Type pop-up menu.

④ Enter in values in the Top, Left, Bottom and Right fields as required.

⑤ Click OK.

Running text around a cutout image

You can run text around images which are cut-out against white backgrounds. The text follows the outline of the cutouts rather than the edges of the picture boxes in which they are contained (see Figure 9.11). The two simplest ways to do this are to choose either the Auto Image or Non-White Areas types of runaround. Auto Image suffices for most cutouts but if a cutout has subtle edges you may wish to edit the path the text runs around directly on the page. In such cases you should choose Non-White Areas.

Alternatively, if you have specified a clipping path for an image (see *Creating a clipping path*, page 131), choose the runaround type Same as clipping.

① With either the Item tool or Content tool active, select the overlaying picture box.

② Choose Runaround... from the Item menu. The Runaround set of controls will be displayed (see Figure 9.12).

Figure 9.11 Text automatically running around the edges of a cutout image

③ Choose Auto Image, Non-White Areas or Same as clipping from the Type pop-up menu.

④ Enter a value in the Outset field. A value other than zero distances the text from the edge of the cutout.

⑤ Enter values in each of the three Tolerance fields; the higher the noise value, the more the control will ignore image blemishes in white backgrounds; the higher the smoothness value, the less it will follow minor 'crevices' in edges; the higher the threshold value, the more it will ignore tonal differences describing edges. The Noise and Threshold options are not available when Same as clipping is chosen.

⑥ Click OK.

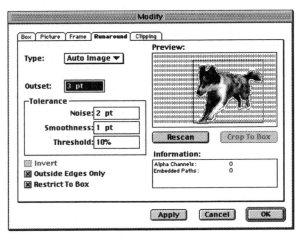

Figure 9.12 Specifying text to runaround a cutout image

Adjusting the path of a Non-White Areas runaround

① Choose Runaround from the Edit sub-menu of the Item menu. An editable path will be displayed around the image cutout.

② Click-drag the handles on the editable path to alter its position.

③ Hold down [⌘] and click on the path's handles to delete them or click on the path between handles to add new handles.

In Windows use the Control key instead of the Command key.

Figure 9.13 Adjusting the path running around the edges of a cutout image

Creating transparency within images

You can mask off parts of images in QuarkXPress so that their backgrounds become completely transparent. This is a useful technique if you wish to overlay images within a layout as any underlying elements show around their shaped edges.

Images treated this way act as an effective visual foil to squared-up images but they are also a useful way of eliminating unsightly backgrounds.

Masking is achieved through the use of clipping paths which effectively hide areas within an image you wish to be transparent. There is therefore no need for you to white out any areas in originals if you do not wish to.

Clipping paths are necessary because grayscale and colour images are opaque even in their white areas, unlike line images which can have transparent whites, if saved in EPS format.

Figure 9.14 A clipped image overlaying text

Creating a clipping path

① With either the Item tool or Content tool active, select the overlaying picture box.

② Choose Clipping... from the Item menu. The Clipping set of controls will be displayed (see Figure 9.15).

③ Choose Non-White from the Type pop-up menu if you wish to mask off – clip – the white background of an image.

④ Enter an Offset value. This affects how far the path is positioned away from the edge of the image profile or embedded path. A figure of –0.1 would slightly clip into tonal regions of the image.

⑤ Uncheck or untick Restrict to Box to ensure that the edges of the picture box do not affect text runaround, if specified.

⑥ Click Crop to Box if you wish the edge of the picture box to limit the size of the path (clip Rescan if you wish to undo this command).

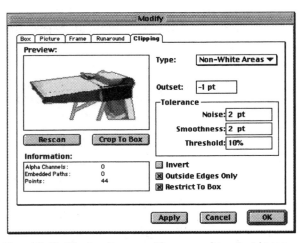

Figure 9.15 Clipping the non-white areas of a cutout image

⑦ Enter values in each of the three Tolerance fields; the higher the noise value, the more the control will ignore image blemishes in backgrounds; the higher the smoothness value, the less it will follow minor 'crevices' in edges; the higher the threshold value, the more it will ignore tonal differences describing edges.

⑧ Click OK.

⑨ You now need to make the picture box transparent by either setting a None box colour or by choosing a Runaround setting other than Item.

❗ If the controls appear not to be working properly, return the setting in the Type field to Item, then do the same in the Runaround set of controls. Then start again in the Clipping set of controls.

File formats explained

QuarkXPress will accept a multitude of file formats, including TIFF, EPS, JPEG, Photo CD and PICT .

TIFF

Scanned images are often saved in TIFF (Tagged Image File Format). This format was originally developed by Microsoft and Aldus and has become a standard worldwide. It can be used to save bilevel, grayscale, RGB images up to 48-bit and CMYK images in 24-bit.

TIFF files do not embed themselves within a document – they're tagged – so you need to keep the original files for outputting purposes.

EPS

Vectored drawn images are usually saved in Encapsulated PostScript (EPS), as are scanned images containing PostScript elements. This format was originally developed by Altsys; it is generic and comes in many forms. Drawings produced in Macromedia FreeHand and Adobe Illustrator, for instance, are saved in this format. It can be used to save bilevel, grayscale, RGB and CMYK colour images in 24-bit.

Like TIFF files, EPS files do not embed themselves within your document so you need to keep the original files for outputting purposes. As they are substantially larger than TIFFs – about a third again in size – it's best to avoid this format for bitmapped images unless you really need its features.

JPEG

Scanned images are often saved in JPEG (Joint Photographic Experts Group) format. This format was developed for the newspaper publishing industry and has become a worldwide standard for transmitting images by modem. It can be used to save bilevel, grayscale, RGB and CMYK colour images in 24-bit.

Because this file format decimates data it's not recommended for normal production work.

Photo CD

This format is specific to Kodak and at present cannot be used to save images onto Macintoshes and PCs. There are several versions of Photo CD but the main one is Master Photo CD for 35 mm. It's used to save YCC colour images in 24-bit, in an image pack of five different resolutions.

PICT File

Vectored drawings/charts and scans can be saved in PICT. This is Apple's native format and it uses the same routines as the software that draws the Macintosh screen. It can be used to save bilevel, grayscale and RGB colour images up to 24-bit.

PICT files always embed themselves in their entirety within the document so you don't need to keep the original files for output.

File format	RGB	CMYK 24-bit	Grayscale 8-bit	Bilevel 1-bit
TIFF	✓	✓	✓	✓
EPS	✓	✓	✓	✓
JPEG	✓	✓	✓	✗
Photo CD	✗	✗	✗	✗
PICT File	✓	✗	✓	✓

Table 9.1 File formats and colour support

Specifying resolutions

Ideally the resolution of scanned images should be roughly twice-linear the halftone screen setting of your final printing device, i.e. if your final printing device is a digital printer and its halftone screen is set at 60 lpi then the resolution of your image should be 120 ppi (dpi) or thereabouts.

Most offset-litho work will be screened at between 100 and 200 lpi, the exact pitch depending on the surface smoothness of the paper to be printed on. Silkscreen work will usually be screened at no more than 100 lpi. Your printing company will be able to advise you on the halftone screen ruling for specific jobs.

If you are scanning images for temporary use only and you plan to replace the images later in the production process, the image resolution need only be 72 ppi (dpi). This will give you acceptable on-screen display and basic proof quality whilst keeping file sizes to the minimum. If you are outputting using a stochastic or other type of dithered screen, set the image resolution to 300 ppi (dpi). If your printing device prints in continuous tone set the image resolution to match the device's outputting resolution, which will probably be between 300 and 400 ppi (dpi).

▲ Always ask your printer for the screen size they propose to use for your job and inform the bureau of the size before they imageset your document.

Storing images

You can store items you use frequently within documents in a library for ease of access. Such items may include logos, pictures and text items. Libraries can contain grouped, locked and layered items: in fact, all QuarkXPress items whatever their attributes.

Creating a library

① Choose Library... from the New sub-menu in the File menu. The New Library directory dialog box will be displayed (see Figure 9.16).

② Name the library.

③ Use the Directory dialog box controls to locate a folder in which to save the new library.

④ Click Create. The Library palette will be displayed.

Figure 9.16 Library palette ready to store items

Opening an existing library

① Choose Open... from the File menu. The Open dialog box will be displayed.

② Use the Directory dialog box controls to locate the library.

③ Click Open. The Library palette will be displayed.

Placing items in the library

① With the Item tool active, click-drag any item from the document into the Library palette. Park the item as indicated by the twin arrows.

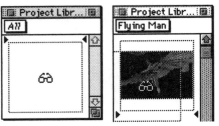

Figure 9.17 Dragging a copy of an item into the Library palette

② Double-click the parked item. The Library Entry dialog box will be displayed.

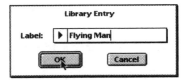

Figure 9.18 Naming a library entry

③ Name the item in the Label field. Click OK.

Taking copies from an open library

The library shows at any one time all stored items, unlabelled items or named items.

① Choose an item from the pop-up menu in the Library palette. If the item is not listed, choose Unlabelled. Unnamed items will then be displayed in the palette.

② With either the Content tool or the Item tool selected, click-drag the item from the Library palette onto the document page.

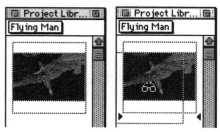

Figure 9.19 Dragging a copy of an item out of the Library palette

✦ Images held in the library maintain their links with original external files and these links are maintained when copies are taken from the library, as if they had been imported directly.

Summary

- **Two types of images** Images within a document can be either vector or bitmapped.

- **Integrating images** Where possible, use the standard 'Get Picture' method for importing all images.

- **Maintaining image quality** Try to avoid re-scaling bitmapped images to more than 165%.

- **Manipulating images** Images should be manipulated within an image editing program, such as Adobe Photoshop, rather than within QuarkXPress.

- **Creating image transparency** White areas within images can be made transparent through the use of clipping paths.

- **Running type around images** Type can run around the edge of a box, cutout image or a clipping path.

- **Using the library** Store regularly-used images, such as logos and photographs, in the library.

using colours

In this chapter you will learn:
- about the existing palette of colours
- how to add new colours
- how to apply colour
- how to manage colour
- how to register colour

The existing palette of colours

Ten basic colours already exist within a QuarkXPress document. These colours are:

- the four process colours: cyan, magenta, yellow and black (CMYK)
- the three RGB colours: red, green and blue
- white (representing white paper)
- registration (for registration and trim marks)
- none (transparent)

The CMYK colours are the process colours used by desktop printers and printing presses to reproduce full colour photographs or illustrations. They are also used as a basis for creating new colours.

Figure 10.1 The ten colours shown in the Colours palette

These colours, apart from the yellow and black, are a bit harsh unmixed, so don't use them individually in colouring work unless you really have to.

The RGB colours are intended for multimedia or other work confined to monitors so it is best to avoid these too.

White represents the colour of the paper you are printing on, whether it's pure white or not. Boxes, by default, have an opaque white background, so when they are placed over other items, the 'white' paper is exposed. If you wish to print white for silkscreen purposes, create a new pale colour (any colour will do) and specify it as a spot colour. You can then inform your printer that this colour represents white and they will then use a white ink when screening the colour.

The colour described as 'none' is transparent. If boxes are given a 'none' background and placed over other items, the underlying items will show through. Don't make boxes transparent for the sake of it, as outputting times are significantly increased if you have a large number of boxes specified this way.

Adding new colours

① Choose Colours... from the Edit menu. The Colours for... dialog box will be displayed (see Figure 10.2). Click New. The Edit Colour dialog box will be displayed (see Figure 10.3).

② Either: leave unchecked or unticked Spot Colour if you wish the new colour to print as a spot colour.

Or: check or tick Spot Colour if you wish the colour to be reproduced using the process colours (CMYK).

Figure 10.2 The Colours for... dialog box

If you are not sure which option to specify, move to the next step and come back to this step later.

If you are only wishing to print a document on a composite grayscale or colour printer, either setting will produce results.

③ Choose either CMYK or Pantone from the Model pop-up menu.

④ Complete the steps under the following CMYK model and Pantone model headings.

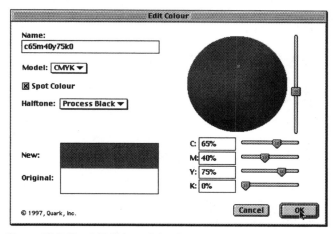

Figure 10.3 The Edit Colour dialog box

! CMYK in the Model pop-up menu refers to the colour model used for creating a colour and not to the way a colour will be reproduced by QuarkXPress.

▲ Check or tick Spot Colour for printed matter using only two or three colours, or as an additional colour to the process colours, when a process equivalent is not accurate enough. Uncheck or untick Spot Colour for printed matter already incorporating full colour photographs and/or illustrations, unless a process equivalent is not accurate enough. Every spot colour in addition to the process colours used for the full colour work will substantially increase printing costs.

✛ Spot colours are printed as a separate ink. Process separated colours (non-spot colours) are printed using the CMYK colours, whichever colour model is selected.

CMYK model

① Type a name in the Name field. It will not be possible for you to save a new colour unless you give it a name.

② Either: enter % values in the Cyan, Magenta, Yellow and Black fields.

Or: click-drag the sliders to the right of the % fields.

Whichever method you use, a dot will move around on the colour wheel and the colour mix will be displayed in the New panel.

③ Click OK. Click Save.

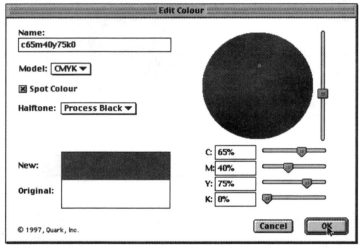

Figure 10.4 Mixing a colour using percentages of cyan, magenta and yellow

▲ When you name a CMYK colour you can give it a descriptive name, such as Poppy, or give it a name describing its composition, such as c65m40y75k0.

Always refer to a book of process colours when choosing colours, as the colours on your monitor will be misleading. Process colour books can be obtained from most printing companies.

Pantone model

① Leave the Name field blank as it will be filled in automatically when you choose a colour.

② Either: click on a swatch in the window. Use the scroll bars to view the full colour range.

Or: enter a known reference number in the Pantone No. field.

The colour mix will be displayed in the New box and the name automatically entered into the Name box.

③ Click OK. Click Save.

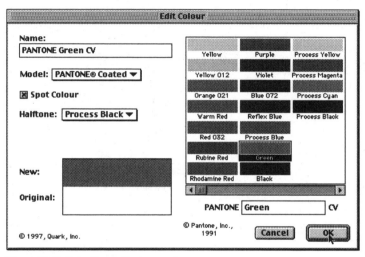

Figure 10.5 Selecting a Pantone colour

❗ Avoid altering a given Pantone name, unless Spot Colour is unchecked or unticked. Otherwise any imported images using the same Pantone colour will create an additional film quite unnecessarily.

▲ Always refer to a book of Pantone colours when choosing colours as the colours on your monitor will be misleading. Pantone colour books can be purchased from graphic art suppliers.

✚ Pantone colours (apart from the fluorescent and metallic colours) are mixed using a limited range of basic colours. By choosing a Pantone swatch for a spot colour, you can be assured that the printer will be able to provide a true colour match.

Applying colours

You can apply colour to text, paragraph rules, lines, box backgrounds and frames, line and grayscale pictures.

Colouring paragraph rules

① Select the paragraph or paragraphs with the rules.

② Choose Rules... from the Style menu. The Rules set of controls will be displayed (see Figure 10.6).

③ Choose options from the Colour and Shade pop-up menus.

④ Click Apply to preview the colour change. Click OK to implement the colour change.

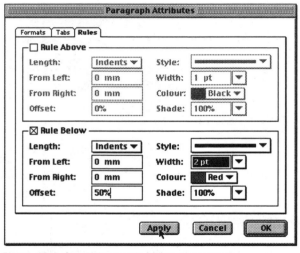

Figure 10.6 Specifying a rule below a paragraph

Colouring and shading box frames

You can use a drag-and-drop technique to alter the colour of box frames using the Colours palette, provided at least one box is selected. Shade adjustments however are restricted to selected boxes. Alternatively you can alter the frame colour and shade of selected boxes within the Frame set of controls.

① With either the Item tool or Content tool active, select a text or picture box.

Either:

② choose Show Colours from the View menu. The Colours palette will be displayed.

③ Click the left-hand Frame icon at the top of the palette (see Figure 10.7).

④ Either: click on a colour name.

Or: click-drag a colour swatch over the frame of an item. The frame will temporarily take on the colour of the swatch. Release the mouse button to apply the colour. Move the swatch away from an item if you do not wish to alter its colour.

⑤ Choose an option from the % (Shade) pop-up menu.

Or:

② choose Frame... from the Item menu. The Frame set of controls will be displayed. Choose options from the Colour and Shade pop-up menus.

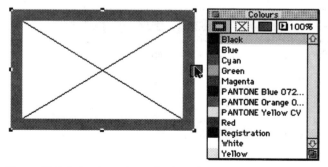

Figure 10.7 Colouring a frame by dragging a swatch from the Colour palette

Colouring and shading boxes

You can use the same drag-and-drop technique mentioned on the previous page to alter the colour of boxes. Alternatively you can alter the colour and shade of selected boxes within the Box set of controls.

① With either the Item tool or Content tool active, select a text or picture box.

Either:

② choose Show Colours from the View menu. The Colours palette will be displayed.

③ Click the right-hand Box icon at the top of the palette (see Figure 10.8).

④ Either: click on a colour name.

Or: click-drag a colour swatch over the background of an item. The box will temporarily take on the colour of the swatch. Release the mouse button to apply the colour. Move the swatch away from an item if you do not wish to alter its colour.

⑤ Choose an option from the % (Shade) pop-up menu.

Or:

② choose Modify... from the Item menu. The Modify dialog box will be displayed.

③ Click the Box tab.

④ Choose options from the Colour and Shade pop-up menus.

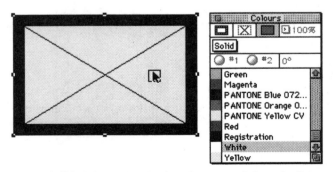

Figure 10.8 Colouring a box by dragging a swatch from the Colour palette

Colouring and shading lines

You can use the same drag-and-drop technique mentioned on the previous pages to alter the colour of lines. Alternatively you can alter the colour and shade of selected lines within the Style menu.

① With either the Item tool or Content tool active, select a line.
Either:

② choose Show Colours from the View menu. The Colours palette will be displayed.

③ The Line icon at the top of the palette will automatically be selected (see Figure 10.9).

④ Either: click on colour name.

Or: click-drag a colour swatch over a line. The line will temporarily take on the colour of the swatch. Release the mouse button to apply a colour. Move the swatch away from a line if you do not wish to alter its colour.

⑤ Select an option in the % (Shade) pop-up menu.

Or:

② choose options from the Colour and Shade sub-menus in the Style menu.

Figure 10.9 Colouring a line by dragging a swatch from the Colour palette

Blending box backgrounds

Colours can be blended in text and picture box backgrounds to meet a variety of design needs.

① With the Item tool active, select a text or empty picture box.

② Choose Show Colours from the View menu. The Colours palette will be displayed.

③ Click the right-hand Background icon at the top of the palette (see Figure 10.10).

④ Choose an option from the Blend pop-up menu.

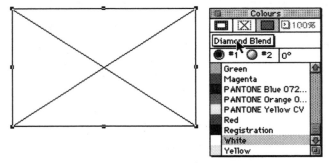

Figure 10.10 Choosing a blend from the Colour palette

⑤ Click the #1 radio button. Click a colour name (not its swatch). This colour will be applied to the background.

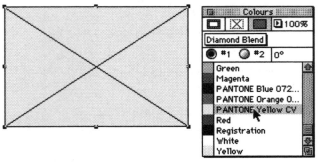

Figure 10.11 Selecting the first blend colour

⑥ Click the #2 radio button. Click another colour name (not its swatch). This second colour will blend with the first colour to create a graduated effect. If you have the Content tool selected, deselect the box to activate blend or select the Item tool.

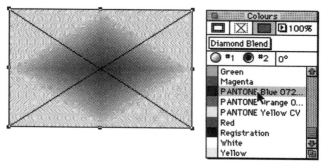

Figure 10.12 Selecting the second blend colour

Colouring and shading images

① With the Content tool active, select an image in a picture box. Either:

② choose Show Colours in the View menu. The Colours palette will be displayed.

③ Click the centre Image icon at the top of the palette.

④ Click on colour name (see Figure 10.13).

⑤ Choose an option from the % (Shade) pop-up menu. Or:

② choose options from the Colour and Shade sub-menus in the Style menu.

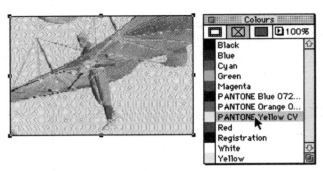

Figure 10.13 Colouring an image

Some picture types which you can colour

| | Image | | Box | |
Type	colour	shade	colour	shade
Bitmapped images:				
Line (1-bit) PICT/TIFF	✓	✓	✓	✓
Grayscale (8-bit) PICT/TIFF	✓	✗	✓	✗
Colour (24-bit) PICT/TIFF	✗	✗	✗	✗
Vector images:				
All colour depths and file types	✗	✗	✗	✗

Colouring and shading text

① With the Content tool active, select the text to be coloured.
Either:

② choose Show Colours from the View menu. The Colours palette will be displayed.

③ Click the centre Text icon at the top of the palette (see Figure 10.14).

④ Click on a colour name and select an option from the % (Shade) pop-up menu.
Or:

② choose options from the Colour and Shade sub-menus in the Style menu.

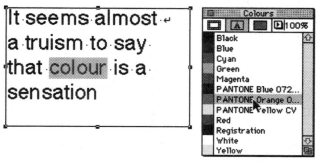

Figure 10.14 Colouring text by selecting a colour from the Colour palette

Managing colours

Basing colours on existing colours

① Choose Colours... from the Edit menu. The Colours for... dialog box will be displayed.

② Select a colour in the Colours list. Click Duplicate.

③ Alter the CMYK mixes or choose another Pantone colour in the same way as you create a colour from scratch.

The New and Old boxes will display the colours for comparison purposes.

④ Type in a new name in the Name field (for CMYK model only). The Pantone name will be amended automatically when you choose a new colour.

⑤ Click OK. Click Save.

▲ Use this approach when you wish to create a colour that will work well with an existing colour.

Amending colours

① Choose Colours... from the Edit menu. The Colours for... dialog box will be displayed.

② Select a colour in the Colours list. Click Edit.

③ Alter the CMYK mixes or choose another Pantone colour in the same way as you create a colour from scratch.

The New and Old boxes will display any colour change for comparison purposes.

④ Click OK. Click Save.

Copying colours from other documents

① Choose Colours... from the Edit menu. The Colours for... dialog box will be displayed.

② Click Append. The Append Colours directory dialog box will be displayed.

③ Locate the document (with the colours) in the Append Colours directory dialog box.

④ Click Open. The colours will be added to the Colours list.

⑤ Click Save.

Registering colours

Hairline gaps can sometimes appear between coloured items when documents are printed on printing presses. This is due to colour mis-registration.

QuarkXPress automatically compensates for such mis-registration by slightly overlapping abutted colours.

Trapping, the term used to describe this process, is applied by QuarkXPress only when files are colour-separated for output to film. No trapping takes place when documents are printed on composite grayscale and colour printers so there's no need to worry about trapping settings when outputting on these devices.

You can enter trapping settings yourself in the Trapping set of controls in the Document Preferences for... dialog box or you can let the bureau handle this for you. Any settings must be agreed by your printer who alone knows the optimum trapping amounts for individual documents.

Preparing items for trapping

Automatic trapping only takes place if items are considered by QuarkXPress to be overlapping. If you do not intend items to touch, ensure there is a small gap between them, otherwise trapping may appear to butt the items together.

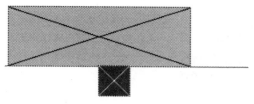

Figure 10.15 Snapping coloured items against a common ruler guide

Overlapping coloured items

Either:

• position coloured items so they are very slightly overlapping.
Or:

• snap coloured items to a common ruler guide.

Summary

• **Ensuring colour fidelity** Always refer to colour reference books when creating new colours.

• **Choosing the right model** Use either the CMYK or one of the Pantone models to create colours.

• **Printing with special inks** Check or tick Spot Colour if you wish a colour to be printed as a special ink on a printing press.

• **Working fast** Use the Colours palette to apply colours quickly to items, text and images.

• **Shading colours** Specify percentage values of colours to tint items, text and images.

• **Avoiding mis-registration when printing** Discuss trapping with your bureau if you are planning to imageset a coloured document.

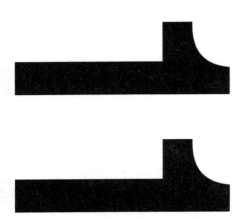

improving the appearance of your work

In this chapter you will learn:
- about hyphenating words
- how to remove widows and orphans
- how to improve readability
- how to adjust word and letter spacing
- how to clean up text

Hyphenating words

Both justified text with overwide word spacing and unjustified text with very ragged line lengths can look unsightly. Such 'horrors' can be reduced through the judicious use of hyphenation. Hyphenation can be inserted automatically or you can do it manually.

Automatic hyphenation is controlled by the Standard H&J by default, is global and does not differentiate between different alignments. For this reason you should turn it off.

Once this has been done, you can hyphenate words yourself by using special discretionary hyphens and/or create your own hyphenated H&J and apply it on a paragraph by paragraph basis.

Disabling auto hyphenation

① Choose H&Js... from the Edit menu. The H&Js for... dialog box will be displayed (see Figure 11.2).

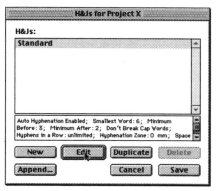

Figure 11.1 Accessing the Standard H&J

② Select Standard in the H&Js list and click Edit. The Edit Hyphenation & Justification dialog box will be displayed.

③ Uncheck or untick Auto Hyphenation.

④ Click OK. Click Save.

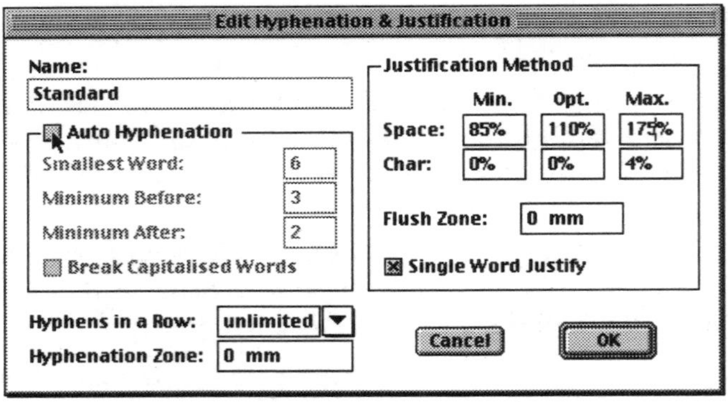

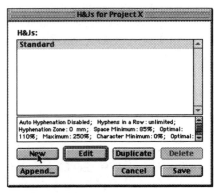

Figure 11.2 Disabling Auto Hyphenation for the Standard H&J

Creating an H&J with auto hyphenation

You can create H&Js with different settings to those of the Standard H&J. For instance, if you wish to automatically hyphenate selected texts, create a special H&J with auto hyphenation enabled.

① Choose H&Js... from the Edit menu. The H&Js for... dialog box will be displayed (see Figure 11.3).

Figure 11.3 Creating a new H&J

② Click New. The Edit Hyphenation & Justification dialog box will be displayed (see Figure 11.4).

③ Enter a name in Name field, such as Auto On.

④ Check or tick Auto Hyphenation.

⑤ Click OK. Click Save.

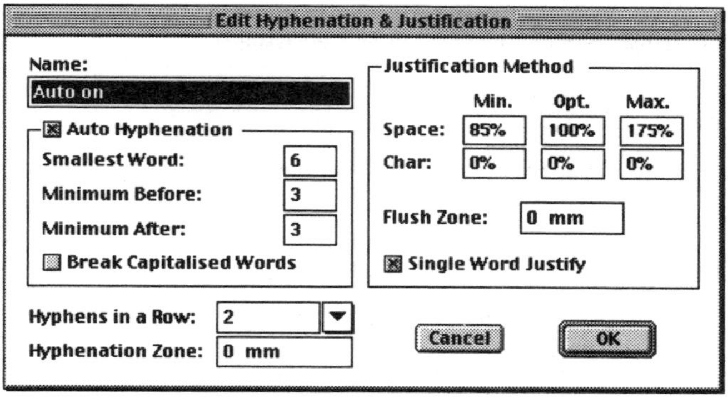

157
improving the appearance
of your work
11

Edit Hyphenation & Justification

Name:
Auto on

☒ Auto Hyphenation
Smallest Word: 6
Minimum Before: 3
Minimum After: 3
☐ Break Capitalised Words

Hyphens in a Row: 2
Hyphenation Zone: 0 mm

Justification Method

	Min.	Opt.	Max.
Space:	85%	100%	175%
Char:	0%	0%	0%

Flush Zone: 0 mm

☒ Single Word Justify

Cancel   OK

Figure 11.4 Creating an auto-hyphenated H&J

Hyphenating locally

Break the first word in each line immediately following an over-spaced or short line using special discretionary hyphens. Unlike ordinary hyphens, these hyphens automatically disappear if a word no longer needs to be broken as a result of subsequent editing work.

Inserting discretionary hyphens

① Position the insertion point within the first word of a line.

② Press ⌘ + - . The word will hyphenate if sufficient space is available in the line above to accommodate the part word.

In Windows use the Control key instead of the Command key.

③ If nothing happens, position the insertion point further left in the word and try step 2 again.

Gaining advice on where to hyphenate

① Position the insertion point within the word.

② Choose Suggested Hyphenation... from the Utilities menu. The Suggested Hyphenation box will be displayed with possible hyphen positions.

▲ Try to avoid hyphenating words within unjustified alignments as hyphens can often look worse than the ragged lines they replace.

Short captions, and text areas composed of mainly short lines and, maybe many names (such as catalogue entries) should always be unhyphenated and unjustified (either with left, centred or right alignments).

Applying an H&J

① Select a paragraph or paragraphs.

② Choose Formats... from the Style menu. The Formats set of controls will be displayed (see Figure 11.5).

③ ⸤Alt⸥-click Apply if it's not already emboldened.

④ Select an option from the H&J pop-up menu.

⑤ Click OK to implement the settings.

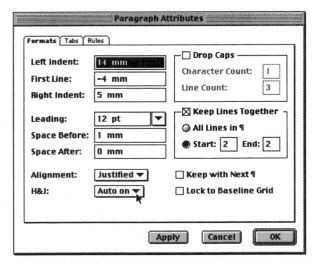

Figure 11.5 Applying an H&J to a paragraph

Removing widows and orphans

Removing widows in paragraphs

Widows are short lines (strictly 6 characters or less) at ends of paragraphs. Because of their short length they sometimes can make text look a bit untidy. Their removal not only neatens text but also reduces the numbers of lines in a text box, which may or may not be beneficial.

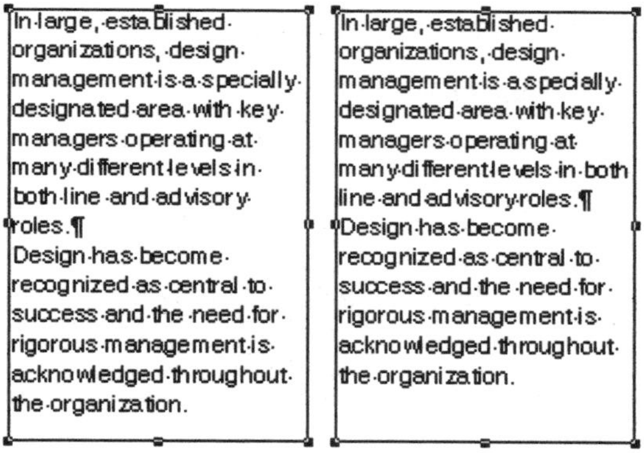

Figure 11.6 Paragraph with widow (left); with widow removed (right)

Removing widows without editing text

① With the Content tool active, select the whole paragraph.

② Choose Track... from the Style menu and enter a figure of up to −5. If the tracking is currently a positive figure, say 8, apply a tracking figure of up to 5 units less, such as 3.

③ Click OK.

Avoiding orphans at column extremities

Orphans are last lines of paragraphs positioned by chance at top and bottoms of text boxes. If they are short in length they can upset the visual alignment of columns, making it appear that the columns are not horizontally aligned.

Like widows, they can also look untidy so it's best where possible to prevent them from appearing. Orphans are eliminated by keeping the first and last two lines of paragraphs together. So

160
improving the appearance
of your work **11**

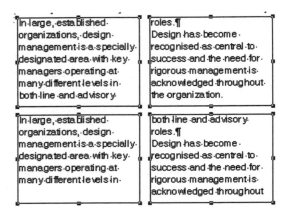

Figure 11.7 Last line of paragraph creates an unsatisfactory first line (top). Preceding line moves up to create a better first line (bottom).

instead of a word appearing at, say, the top of a linked box or column, the line preceding the potential orphan also moves up to the top, thereby providing a first full line of text.

This leaves an empty last line in the previous column which can be filled, if so desired, by adding an additional line in the column by whatever means appropriate.

Figure 11.8 Ensuring that the first and last two lines of paragraphs keep together

Avoiding orphans automatically

① With the Content tool active, select a paragraph or paragraphs.

② Choose Formats... from the Style menu. The Formats set of controls will be displayed (see Figure 11.8).

③ Check or tick Keep Lines Together. Click Start and enter 2 in the Start and End fields.

④ Click OK.

Removing 'rivers' in paragraphs

Rivers are unsightly gaps running more or less vertically in areas of text caused by the incidence of large adjacent words spaces.

Remove 'rivers' by negative tracking – see *Removing widows in paragraphs* (page 159) or by applying local hyphenation – see *Hyphenating locally* (page 157).

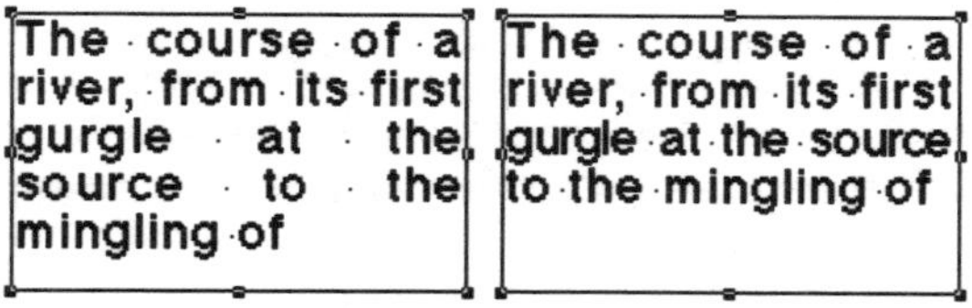

Figure 11.9 Paragraph with unsightly river (left); with river removed (right)

Improving readability

Improving leading

Almost all text is made more readable by the addition of leading. It alters the colour (texture) of text areas and makes the text more accessible.

If you feel paragraphs can be improved through the adjustment of leading, alter the leading locally within paragraphs or, if you have used style sheets in your document, amend the leading within individual style sheets.

Use minimal leading values for very short lines of text, equal to or slightly *greater* than the font size. Also use minimal leading values for large headings, equal to or slightly *less* than the font size.

Lines of eight to ten words in length normally require leading which roughly corresponds to 110% of the font size. Longer lines, of course, require proportionately more leading.

Setting readable line lengths

The optimum number of characters per line of continuous text varies considerably between types of documents. In books, 60–70 would represent a good basis to work from. You can try a larger number of characters per line than this, with generous leading, and it may work; certainly anything above 90 characters per line will be too much. In news articles, between 30 and 45 characters per line is the norm.

Text with a low character count per line tends to look racy, readable and accessible, whilst text with a high character count tends to look more formal and perhaps more imposing, although much depends on other factors.

If you wish to alter the character count in paragraphs, either alter the width of text areas and/or alter the size of fonts. Alter the font size locally within paragraphs or, if you have used style sheets in your document, amend the font size within individual style sheets.

Adjusting word and letter spacing

Maintaining good word and character spacing

Use standard tracking (zero units of track) for normal text areas. Occasionally, some slight closing-up (negative tracking) or slight widening (positive tracking) may be appropriate in text. Ideally, tracking should not vary within a paragraph.

Text in very small font sizes, around 6 or 7 pt, can be slightly widened on occasions to improve legibility. In display sizes, of say 18 pt and above, some slight closing-up (negative tracking) is often desirable, otherwise the work looks too 'gappy'.

Improving spacing in justified alignments

Word and character spacing within justified paragraphs is controlled by the Standard H&J by default and is global. The justification settings have a marked effect on the look of text and should be set to allow for a reasonable amount of variation in word spacing, with limited variation in inter-character spacing.

① Choose H&Js... from the Edit menu. The H&Js for... dialog box will be displayed (see Figure 11.10).

② Select Standard in the H&Js list and click Edit. The Edit Hyphenation & Justification dialog box will be displayed (see Figure 11.11).

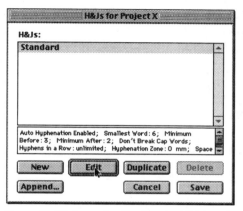

Figure 11.10 Accessing the Standard H&J settings

③ Alter the values in the Justification method fields to match the illustration.

④ Click OK. Click Save.

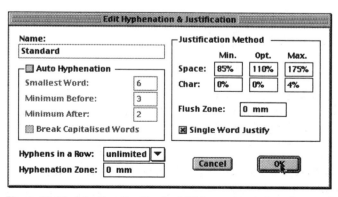

Figure 11.11 Adjusting the Standard H&Js word and character spacing

Improving the spacing between characters

You can correct poor spacing between individual characters within large headings by kerning. You can also create interesting character juxtapositions by the same means. Like tracking, kerning is measured as percentages of an en space. Unkerned inter-character spaces are set at 0.

Figure 11.12 The figures 1 and 9 are too wide apart (top). The figures are kerned to decrease the spacing between them (bottom).

Adjusting inter-character spaces

① Position the insertion point between two characters within a word. The text should not be highlighted in any way.

② Choose Kern... from the Style menu and enter a figure in the Kern dialog box.

A positive figure, such as 5 will widen the inter-character spacing; a negative figure such as –5 will tighten the inter-character spacing.

▲ Only kern badly-spaced characters in very large font sizes, say over 36 pt. It's usually unnecessary to kern smaller sizes as any poor inter-character spacing is less disturbing to the eye.

Cleaning up text

Eliminating typing errors

If you wish to remove all instances of double spaces, spaces before full points and other errors, use the Find/Change function within the Edit menu.

① Select the Content tool but do not select a text box.

② Choose Find/Change... from the Edit menu. The Find/Change dialog box will be displayed (see Figure 11.13).

③ Type in the character(s) to be found in the Find What field and replacement character(s), if any, in the Change To field.

④ Check or tick Document to find and change all text within the document.

⑤ Click Find Next to find the first instance of the character(s) and click Replace if you wish to replace the character(s).

⑥ Click Find Next again and repeat the process until all instances of the characters have been replaced.

⑦ Close the dialog box.

165
improving the appearance
of your work
11

Figure 11.13 Removing all instances of double returns in a document

▲ See Appendix II *Special characters* for the special codes to use in the Find/Change fields.

You can involve text attributes in the Find/Change process. See next section.

Improving font and type style assignment

You can fairly easily alter the assignment of fonts and typestyles within your document. You may, for example, have formatted text using the bold type style rather than using the bold variant of a font. Because it's always preferable to use a font variant (such as B Century Old Style Bold), you may wish to globally replace all occurences of the emboldened font styles before outputting your document.

① Select the Content tool but do not select a text box.

② Choose Find/Change... from the Edit menu. The Find/Change dialog box will be displayed.

③ Type in any character(s) in the Find What and Change To fields.

④ Uncheck or untick Ignore Attributes.

⑤ Uncheck or untick Text in both panels.

⑥ Check or tick Font in both panels.

⑦ Check or tick Document to change attributes throughout the document.

Specifying which attributes you wish to change

① Choose the font you wish to change in the Font pop-up menu.

② Check or tick Type Style only if you wish to limit the changes to specific styles.

Specifying which attributes you wish to apply

① Choose the font variant you wish to apply in the Font pop-up menu.

② Check or tick Type Style only if you wish to limit the changes to specific styles.

Finding and changing attributes

① Click Find Next to find the first instance of the attributes and click Replace if you wish to change the attributes.

② Click Find Next again and repeat the process until all instances of the characters have been replaced.

③ Close the dialog box.

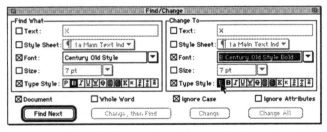

Figure 11.14 Substituting the font B Century Old Style Bold for all instances of the emboldened font Century Old Style

▲ You can combine text and attribute changes in the Find/Change process. Instead of entering any text in the Text fields and unchecking Text, enter in the appropriate text and leave Text checked in both panels. See previous section.

Eliminating wrong fonts

You can easily identify and replace incorrectly-used fonts before outputting your document.

① Choose a scale from the View menu which enables you to read all your document text easily.

② Choose Usage... from the Utilities menu. The Usage dialog box will be displayed. Click the Fonts tab (see Figure 11.15).

167
improving the appearance
of your work
11

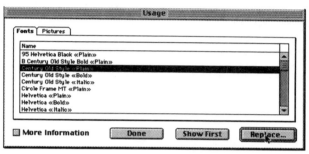

Figure 11.15 Selecting Century Old Style for replacement

③ View the fonts you've used in the Name list. If all your fonts are present and correct, close the dialog box.

If a font is listed which you did not intend to use, follow the next steps.

④ Select the font name. Click Show First and then Show Next if you wish to view instances of the font in use.

⑤ Click Replace... The Replace Font dialog box will be displayed (see Figure 11.16).

⑥ Choose a suitable font from the Replacement Font pop-up menu. Click OK. An Alert box saying 'All occurences of the font "..." will be replaced by "...". OK to replace?' will be displayed.

⑦ Click OK if you wish to proceed. Click Cancel if you wish to return to the Replace Font dialog box and choose another replacement font.

⑧ Repeat steps 4 to 7 until all the wrong fonts have been replaced.

⑨ Click Done.

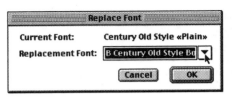

Figure 11.16 Choosing B Century Old Style Bold as a replacement font

▲ The Usage dialog box is one reference point for listing fonts for your bureau (if you do not use Collect for Output).

Summary

- **Maintaining textural consistency** Maintain an even texture in all text areas.
- **Breaking words** Apply hyphenation locally within most documents.
- **Keeping text neat looking** Remove widows and orphans and unsightly word spacing as a matter of course.
- **Limiting the use of hyphens** Where possible, avoid hyphenating text which is left, centred or right aligned.
- **Spacing headings** Kern large text if the inter-character spacing is too uneven.
- **Apply generous leading** Use generous leading for paragraphs with long lines set in small font sizes.
- **Correcting typos** Use the Find/Change function to remove typing errors.
- **Replacing wrong fonts** Incorrectly specified fonts can be globally changed within the Fonts set of controls.

preparing files for printing

In this chapter you will learn:
- how to output from another computer
- how to print documents
- how to shorten proofing times
- about working with OPI
- how to copy files for output
- what a bureau needs to know

QuarkXPress documents can be printed using desktop printers or large digital colour presses (such as those made by Canon, Indigo and Xeikon). They can also be imageset at a bureau to produce bromide or film for subsequent photo litho printing.

Whichever method of output you employ, picture links need to be checked prior to final output and if you are outputting from a computer other than your own, you will also need to check the font usage.

Outputting from another computer

Checking picture links

When you include images in a QuarkXPress document, links are automatically established between individual images within your document and their originals.

When you output your document, QuarkXPress uses the data in the original files to reproduce the images, unless the images have been saved in PICT format, in which case it uses the embedded file. If it's unable to locate and use the original files, QuarkXPress will use the data in the embedded images for reproduction purposes. Reproduction by this means is inferior but may be adequate for printing or for proofing purposes.

If links between the images and their original files are inadvertently broken, they can easily be re-established using the Picture Usage dialog box. It's important, in any case, to check the status of all links on completion of a document, whether or not you think any links are broken.

Checking picture linkage

① Choose Usage... from the Utilities menu. The Usage dialog box will be displayed. Click the Picture tab (see Figure 12.1).

② Look at the status column for each picture. The status will be OK, Modified or Missing.

If the status in all cases is OK, there is no need for you to do anything so click Done to close the dialog box.

If the status of any picture is Missing, select the file name and click Update... The Find "..." directory dialog box will be displayed. Locate and select the missing picture file using the directory dialog box controls. Click Open.

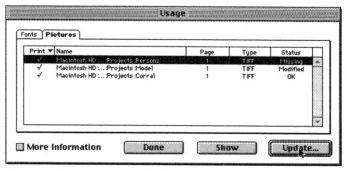

Figure 12.1 Reconnecting a missing image

If the status of any picture is Modified, select the file name and click Update. An alert dialog box saying 'OK to update "..."?' will be displayed.

③ Close the dialog box.

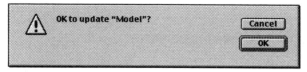

Figure 12.2 Alert dialog box

✦ OK status means the document is properly linked to an unmodified picture file. Modified status means the document is properly linked to a modified picture file. Missing status means the document is no longer linked to the picture file originally imported. This is usually because the file has since been moved or renamed.

Font usage

When your document is output, QuarkXPress uses the fonts loaded on the outputting computer. If your document uses non-system fonts, QuarkXPress will ask for suitable substitute fonts if the specified fonts are not available. This almost invariably occurs when documents are output at a bureau.

If you restrict your font usage to the Macintosh or Windows system fonts, you should have no problem in this regard. Obviously you won't be able to restrict yourself to these fonts for most jobs. So if you are planning to imageset your document and you wish to use fonts other than System fonts, use only Adobe Type 1 fonts.

Where possible, avoid Truetype fonts on either system as they perform less reliably on PostScript devices. Purely bitmap (non-outline) fonts should also be avoided.

Checking font usage

① Choose Usage... from the Utilities menu. The Usage dialog box will be displayed.

② Click the Font tab (see Figure 12.3).

③ View the fonts you've used in the Name list.

④ Click Done to close the dialog box.

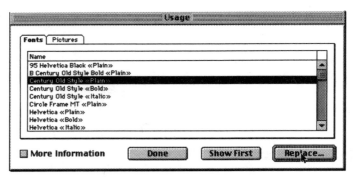

Figure 12.3 One place to view fonts used in a document

▲ The Usage dialog box is a useful reference point when listing fonts for your bureau (if you do not use Collect for Output).

Printing documents

Logging into a printer

On the Macintosh

① Choose Chooser from the Apple menu. The Chooser dialog box will be displayed (see Figure 12.4).

② Click the driver of the printer you wish to use, in the top left window.

③ Select a zone (if your printer is networked) in the bottom left window.

④ Click the printer listed in the right window.

⑤ Click the Close box.

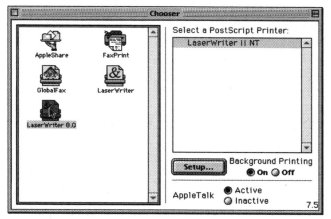

Figure 12.4 Selecting a printer on a Macintosh

❗ Ensure that AppleTalk is active in the Chooser, otherwise your computer will not be able to communicate with the printer.

In Windows

① Choose Print... from the File menu. The Print dialog box will be displayed.

② Choose a driver from the Printer pop-up menu.

③ Click the Capture Settings button.

Previewing a document

- Choose Hide Guides and Hide Invisibles from the View menu. If an item is already hidden the word Show will replace the word Hide so there is no need to choose the command.

Printing a document

- Choose Print... from the File menu. The Print dialog box will be displayed. Note that the sets of controls in this dialog box may differ from our illustration.

Setting the way pages print on the page

① Click the Document tab (see Figure 12.5).

② Uncheck or untick Spreads for printing pages on separate sheets of paper. Check or tick Spreads for printing adjacent pages together on the same sheet of paper. If you select the latter option, ensure the paper size and scale is set to accommodate two pages side by side. The page size is chosen in the Page Setup dialog box and the orientation is selected within the same box or within the Setup controls.

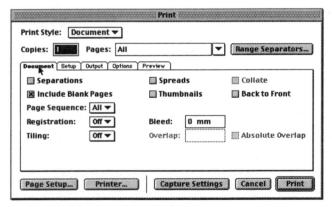

Figure 12.5 The document set of controls

③ Uncheck or untick Collate if you wish multiple copies of pages to be printed together. This is the more efficient, faster way to print but will mean you will have to collate your documents by hand. Check or tick Collate if you wish sets of documents to be printed together. This is the less efficient, slower way to print.

④ Choose either Centred or Off Centre in the Registration pop-up menu if you wish trim marks to print. Otherwise select Off.

The above settings will be saved with your document.

Specifying the page setup

① Click the Setup tab (see Figure 12.6).

② Choose your printer from the Printer Description pop-up menu.

③ Choose the paper size from the Paper Size pop-up menu.

④ Enter a value in the Reduce or Enlarge field. This option may not be available on a non-PostScript printer.

⑤ Click an Orientation option to suit your document.

The above settings will be saved with your document.

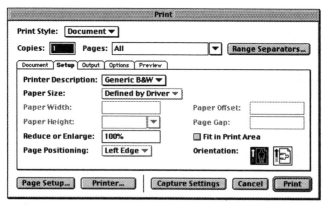

Figure 12.6 This set of controls mirrors those of your printer's Page Setup

Accessing your printer's own page setup controls

① Click the Page Setup... button. Your printer's setup controls will be displayed (see Figure 12.7).

In Windows click the Properties... button

② Alter the settings as required.

③ Click OK.

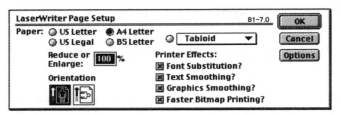

Figure 12.7 The full set of controls specific to your printer is accessed from the print dialog box

Setting the way colour prints on grayscale printers

① Click the Output tab (see Figure 12.8).

② Check or tick Greyscale from the Print Colours pop-up menu in the Output if you are printing a coloured document on a black and white (greyscale) printer. Otherwise leave alone.

The above setting will be saved with your document.

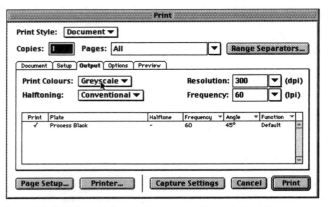

Figure 12.8 This set of controls governs the output of images

Specifying which pages are to print

① Enter the number of copies of each page required in the Copies field.

② Under Pages, enter All or either a sequence of pages, such as 35-39, or non-continuous pages, such as 7,28-29,46.

③ Click Print.

Printing large document pages

If you are printing document pages larger than the paper in your printer, and you wish to print the pages full size, it's possible to print each page in sections. Once the sections are printed, you can tape them together to recreate each page.

① Position the Ruler Origin at the top left corner of the image area to be printed. See *Moving the ruler zero points* (page 31).

② Choose Print... from the File menu. The Print dialog box will be displayed (see Figure 12.9). Note that the contents of this dialog box may differ from our illustration.

③ Choose Manual from the Tiling pop-up menu. The current position of the ruler origin will determine the top left corner of the image area to be printed.

④ Click Print.

⑤ Reposition the ruler origin so that it is at the top left corner of the next area of the document page you wish to print.

⑥ Choose Print... again from the File menu. The Print dialog box will be displayed.

⑦ Click Print.

⑧ Repeat steps 5–7 until all the areas of the page have been printed.

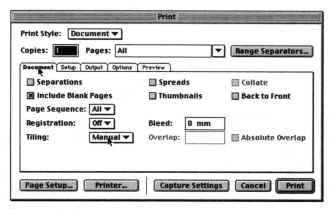

Figure 12.9 Choosing Manual as a tiling option

Shortening proofing times

If your document includes a large number of images, printing times will inevitably be long. You can shorten printing times by omitting images or printing them at a low resolution.

Omitting or printing all images at low resolution

① Choose Print... from the File menu. The Print dialog box will be displayed (see Figure 12.10). Note that the sets of controls in this dialog box may differ from Figure 12.10.

② Click the Options tab.

③ Either: choose Rough from the Output pop-up menu to omit images within picture boxes.

Or: choose Low Resolution from the Output pop-up menu to print images at 72 dpi (ppi).

④ Make other settings, as necessary, in the Document, Setup and Output dialog boxes.

⑤ Click Print.

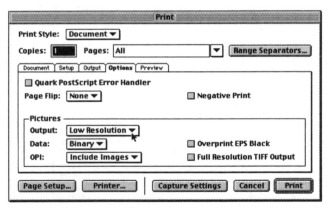

Figure 12.10 Choosing Low Resolution output to speed printing times

Omitting selected images and picture boxes

① Select individual picture boxes with either the Content tool or Item tool active.

② Choose Modify... from the Item menu. The Box set of controls will be displayed.

③ Check or tick Suppress Printout to omit image only.

④ Click OK.

Omitting selected images

① Choose Usage... from the Utilities menu.

② Click the Picture tab.

③ Remove the tick to the left of listed picture by clicking on it.

④ Click Done.

Omitting all TIFFs and/or EPS when printing

① Choose Print... from the File menu. The Print dialog box will be displayed (see Figure 12.11). Note that the sets of controls in this dialog box may differ from Figure 12.11.

② Click the Options tab.

③ Choose either Omit TIFF or Omit TIFF & EPS in the OPI pop-up menu.

④ Click Print.

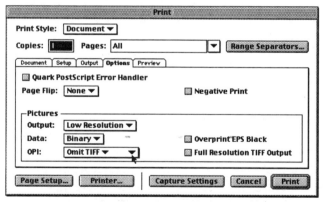

Figure 12.11 Omitting TIFFs to speed printing times

Working with OPI

Open Press Interface (OPI) enables the automatic substitution of low-resolution TIFF and EPS images for high-resolution versions when outputting within 'high-end' pre-press systems.

One of the key benefits of OPI is that it removes the need for you to hold large files on your computer drives.

When images are scanned for OPI, two versions of each image are made, one low-resolution and one high-resolution. The low-resolution images are created for layout purposes; the high-resolution images for outputting purposes. OPI comments (instructions) are included in both files.

When either Omit TIFF or Omit TIFF and EPS is selected in the OPI pop-up menu in the Print dialog box, only the positional, scaling and cropping information of images is sent to the imagesetter.

The OPI interpreter reads the OPI comments in the low-resolution files and makes the substitution.

Omitting the redundant low-resolution picture data speeds processing times and reduces costs.

If OPI is used, it's best to convert those images which are not intended to be substituted for different file formats. For example if only TIFFs are to be substituted, ensure all other files are EPS.

OPI is only suitable for documents containing a large number of images with schedules which allow for all the scanning to take place prior to page layout work.

Using OPI

① For every image in your document, specify:

The document width and height in mm (as in Document setup), or percentage reduction/ enlargement.

Whether it is to be reproduced in line, grayscale or colour.

② Send all prints and transparencies to your bureau for scanning and OPI work. Note that not all bureaux employ OPI technology.

③ Import the low-resolution images you receive from the bureau/printer into your document using the normal Get Picture method.

④ Complete your document production work and submit your document and associated files to your bureau in the usual way.

Copying files for output

If you are proofing, printing or imagesetting your document at a bureau, the bureau will need a final copy of your document and all associated files, unless they have been saved in PICT format.

There are two ways to copy files. One way is to copy them manually to disk. Another way is to use Collect for Output, QuarkXPress's way of automatically copying files to disk. The manual way has one major advantage: you can copy across files in their folders so all your files remain in an organized structure.

In theory, Collect for Output guarantees that all files are copied irrespective of their location on your computer. In the copying and collection process, all the files are brought together into a single folder. Because of this, try to make sure all your images have unique names, otherwise they may be renamed during the collection process.

Collect for Output produces a report in a text file format covering essential document information, Xtensions, fonts, images, style sheets, H&Js, colours, trapping, colour plates and so on. This checklist can be printed out by yourself and your bureau/printer.

Collecting pictures for output

① Choose Collect for Output... from the File menu. The Collect for Output directory dialog box will be displayed.

② Name the Report in the name field.

③ Select or create a folder (directory) on the disk in which to copy the QuarkXPress document and all its associated files.

④ Click Collect.

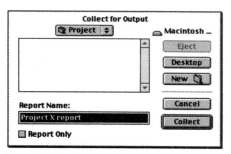

Figure 12.12 Copying a document with linked files into a folder called 'Project'

Copying files to disk on the Macintosh

① Either: insert a double-sided, high density floppy into your disk drive.

Or: mount a larger ejectable disk onto your Desktop.

② Click-drag the folders containing your QuarkXPress document and associated files on your hard drive onto the icon of the floppy or ejectable disk. The files will be copied onto the disk.

③ Click-drag the floppy or ejectable disk icon into the Wastebasket. The floppy or ejectable disk will be ejected/unmounted.

Copying files to disk in Windows

① Either: insert a double-sided, high density floppy into your disk drive.

Or: mount a larger ejectable disk onto your Desktop.

② Click-drag the folders containing your QuarkXPress document and associated files on your hard drive onto the icon of the floppy or ejectable disk. The files will be copied onto the disk.

③ Press the Eject button on the front of the drive. The floppy or ejectable disk will be ejected/unmounted.

What a bureau needs to know

Outputting to bromide

Inform the bureau about the following:

* Document details:
  File name, program version, platform (Macintosh or PC)
* Document Setup details:
  The document page size (in mm)
* Page Setup details:
  Whether 100% scale or % reduction/enlargement
  The half-tone screen ruling (in lpi)

- Print details:
  The pages to be output
  Whether registration marks are required
  Whether adjacent pages are to be printed as spreads
- Material details:
  That bromides are required
- Font details:
  Any non-system fonts used, including font type, foundry's name, font name, variant and typestyle
- Picture details:
  Picture types and number, such as EPS × 5, TIFF × 3.

Outputting to colour proofs

Inform the bureau about the following:
- Document details:
  File name, program version, platform (Macintosh or PC)
- Document Setup details:
  The document page size (in mm)
- Page Setup details:
  Whether 100% scale or % reduction/enlargement
  The size of the paper to be printed on (A4 or larger)
- Print details:
  The pages to be output
  Whether registration marks are required
  Whether adjacent pages are to be printed as spreads
- Process and material details:
  Type of digital colour prints required
- Font details:
  Any non-system fonts used, including font type, foundry's name, font name, variant and typestyle
- Picture details:
  Picture types and number, such as EPS × 5, TIFF × 3.

Outputting to colour separations

Inform the bureau about the following:

- Document details:
  File name, program version, platform (Macintosh or PC)
- Document Setup details:
  The document page size (in mm)
- Page Setup details:
  Whether 100% scale or % reduction/enlargement
  The half-tone screen ruling (in lpi)
- Print details:
  The pages to be output
  That registration and crop marks will be required
  Imagesetter resolution (whether 1270 or 2540 dpi)
  Trapping details
  Number of colours (process and spot colours)
  Whether adjacent pages are to be printed as spreads or imposed for printing plates. If the latter is proposed, the imposition to be supplied by printer.
- Material details:
  That film positive or negatives are required, emulsion side down or up.
- Font details:
  Any non-system fonts used, including font type, foundry's name, font name, variant and typestyle, such as PostScript, Monotype, Gill Bold, Italic
- Picture details:
  Picture types and number, such as EPS × 5, TIFF × 3.
- Colour details:
  The process/spot colours used, such as cyan, magenta, yellow, black and Pantone Reflex Blue.

Summary

- **Checking pictures and fonts** Always check picture and font usage when completing a document.

- **Printing faster** Shorten proofing times by printing images at low resolution.

- **Ensuring all files are copied together** Use Collect for Output for copying files to disk.

- **Informing your bureau** Give your bureau all the information they need to imageset a job accurately.

appendix i ■

Measurements

Font sizes

Fonts are sized in points (a unit measuring close to $^1/_{72}$ inch and very roughly one-third of a millimetre). A font size refers to the height of the body of a font and not the printed height (the body height can be seen when text is selected). Thus a 10 pt font has a body height of 10 pt and an overall printed height, from ascender to descender, of fractionally less.

Leading

Leading is also measured in points. Leading refers to the distance from the baseline of one line of type to the next within a paragraph (the baseline is the imaginary line running along the bottom of those letters without descenders, such as an x).

The word 'leading' derives from the slivers of lead used to space out lines of metal type. Leading is usually expressed as the sum of the font size and leading thickness.

When the leading size is the same as the font size, the font is said to be unleaded. When the leading size is smaller, negative leading takes place (this would have been impossible with metal type).

Auto leading is pre-set at 120% of the font size and should only be used when initially sizing fonts or for single lines in text boxes.

Horizontal measures

Margin and gutter measures are normally specified in millimetres and paragraph indents in points. Paragraph indents are
usually based on multiples or divisions of the font size, such as
an em.

Vertical measures

Spaces before and after paragraphs and the offset of paragraph
rules are normally measured in millimetres, points or alternatively, in the case of rules, expressed as a percentage of paragraph spaces. Spaces are usually based on multiples or divisions
of the leading.

Word spaces

Normal word spaces, created using the space bar only, are
approximately 0.5 en wide depending on the font and are subject to enlargement and reduction in justified setting. If you wish
to maintain their width in selected situations, such as beside bullet points, use a fixed word space (see *Special characters*, pages
188 and 192).

✚ An en is equal to half the font size and corresponds roughly to the width of
a lower-case n, from which it derives its name. Thus a 10 pt en is 5 pt wide.

Wider spaces can be inserted using the keyboard. Inserting two
en spaces beside each other creates the wider em space.

✚ An em is equal to the font size and corresponds roughly to the width of a
capital M, from which it derives its name. Thus a 10 pt em is 10 pt wide.

Both en and fixed word spaces maintain their width in justified
setting but are affected by kerning and tracking changes.

appendix ii

Special characters for the Macintosh

Included in this appendix are the most common special characters. There are many more. If there's a character you wish to use and it's not listed, refer to Key Caps in the Apple menu.

If this does not help you, you may need to buy a special font.

Most of the characters are achieved by using the modifier keys together with other keys. These keys – [⌘], [Alt], [Shift] and [Control] – should be held down separately or in various combinations whilst another key is pressed.

Certain key combinations may not work, especially the ones which create accented characters. This could mean you are using a keyboard setting other than the British one. Check the current keyboard setting in the Keyboard Control Panel. This panel is accessed via the Apple menu.

Quotation marks

"	[Alt]+[{ [ ]	opening double quotes
"	[Alt][Shift]+[{ [ ]	closing double quotes
'	[Alt]+[}]]	opening single quote
'	[Alt][Shift]+[}]]	closing single quote

❗ It is only necessary to use the above four sets of commands if Smart Quotes is unchecked or unticked in the Interactive set of controls in the Application Preferences dialog box.

Inch and foot marks

"   [Control] [Shift] + [" ']   Imperial inch mark

'   [Control] + [" ']   Imperial foot mark

‼ It is only necessary to use the above four sets of commands if Smart Quotes is checked or ticked in the Interactive set of controls in the Application Preferences dialog box.

Selected punctuation, characters and symbols

…	[Alt] + [: ;]	ellipsis
•	[Alt] + [* 8]	small bullet point
■	[N] (Zapf Dingbats font)	solid box
□	[N] (Zapf Dingbats, outlined)	outlined box
●	[L] (Zapf Dingbats font)	solid bullet point
○	[L] (Zapf Dingbats, outlined)	outlined bullet point
×	[Alt] + [Y] (Symbol font)	multiplication sign
fi	[Alt] [Shift] + [% 5]	ligature of f and i
fl	[Alt] [Shift] + [^ 6]	ligature of f and l
©	[Alt] + [G]	copyright mark
TM	[Alt] + [@ 2]	trade mark
®	[Alt] + [R]	registered mark
°	[Alt] [Shift] + [* 8]	degree symbol
†	[Alt] + [T]	dagger
€	[Alt] [Shift] + [@ 2]	euro
¢	[Alt] + [$ 4]	cent
¥	[Alt] + [Y]	yen
¿	[Alt] [Shift] + [? /]	opening question mark
¡	[Alt] + [! 1]	opening exclamation mark
/	[Alt] [Shift] + [! 1]	shallow slash for fractions

✚ The set of commands for the Euro character gives the system font. Only available from System 8.5 onwards.

Special characters for the Find/Change dialog box

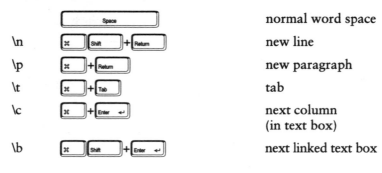

	Space	normal word space
\n	⌘ Shift + Return	new line
\p	⌘ + Return	new paragraph
\t	⌘ + Tab	tab
\c	⌘ + Enter ↵	next column (in text box)
\b	⌘ Shift + Enter ↵	next linked text box

Word spaces

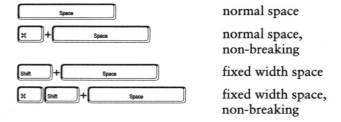

Space	normal space
⌘ + Space	normal space, non-breaking
Shift + Space	fixed width space
⌘ Shift + Space	fixed width space, non-breaking

✚ A non-breaking space ensures that characters either side of it remain together on the same line of text. A fixed width space, unlike a normal space, maintains its width within justified alignments.

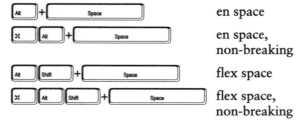

Alt + Space	en space
⌘ Alt + Space	en space, non-breaking
Alt Shift + Space	flex space
⌘ Alt Shift + Space	flex space, non-breaking

✚ A flex space is a user-definable space. Enter 25% (of an em) in the Flex Space Width field in the Character set of controls in the Typographic Preferences for … dialog box for a space approximately half the width of a standard word space. Unfortunately only one flex space setting can be specified within a document.

Page numbers

⌘ + #3   page number code

Text commands

Return	paragraph return
Shift + Return	new line return
⌘ + Return	new line return, discretionary
⌘ + I \	indent following lines
Enter ↵	next column (in text box)
Shift + Enter ↵	next linked text box

Hyphens and dashes

-	–.	hyphen
-	⌘ + –.	hyphen, discretionary
–	Alt + –.	en dash
—	Alt Shift + –.	em dash

Accented letters

ç	Alt + C	cedilla
é	Alt + E, then E or other	acute
è	Alt + ~#, then E or other	grave
ü	Alt + U, then U or other	umlaut
ñ	Alt + N, then N or other	tilde
î	Alt + I, then I or other	circumflex

❗ For all the above six commands, press the Alt key with the letter and then press the appropriate character.

Special characters for Windows

Included in this appendix are the most common special characters. There are many more. If there's a character you wish to use and it's not listed, refer to the Character Map in the Accessories folder. This folder is accessed via the Start menu.

If this does not help you, you may need to buy a special font.

Most of the characters are achieved by using the modifier keys together with other keys. These keys – [Control], [Alt] and [Shift] – should be held down separately or in various combinations whilst another key is pressed.

Quotation marks

"	[Alt] [Shift] +[{ []	opening double quotes
"	[Alt] [Shift] +[}]]	closing double quotes
'	[Alt] +[{ []	opening single quote
'	[Alt] +[}]]	closing single quote

! It is only necessary to use the above four sets of commands if Smart Quotes is unchecked or unticked in the Interactive set of controls in the Application Preferences dialog box.

Inch and foot marks

"	[Control] [Shift] +[" ']	Imperial inch mark
'	[Control] +[" ']	Imperial foot mark

! It is only necessary to use the above four sets of commands if Smart Quotes is checked or ticked in the Interactive set of controls in the Application Preferences dialog box.

Selected punctuation, characters and symbols

...	[Alt] +0133	ellipsis
•	[Alt] [Shift] +[* 8]	small bullet point
■	[N] (Wingdings font)	solid box
□	[N] (Wingdings, outlined)	outlined box
●	[L] (Wingdings font)	solid bullet point

○	⬜L (Wingdings, outlined)	outlined bullet point
×	[Alt]+[Y] (Symbol font)	multiplication sign
©	[Alt][Shift]+[C]	copyright mark
™	[Alt][Shift]+[@₂]	trade mark
®	[Alt][Shift]+[R]	registered mark
°	[Alt]+0176	degree symbol
†	[Alt][Shift]+[T]	dagger
€	[Control][Alt]+[$₄]	euro
¢	[Alt]+0162	cent
¥	[Alt]+0165	yen
¿	[Alt]+0191	opening question mark
¡	[Alt]+0161	opening exclamation mark

✚ The set of commands for the Euro character gives the system font. This currently can be downloaded from Microsoft's web site.

Special characters for the Find/Change dialog box

	type using space bar	normal word space
\n	type as shown	new line
\p	type as shown	new paragraph
\t	type as shown	tab
\c	type as shown	next column (in text box)
\b	type as shown	next linked text box

Word spaces

[Space]	normal space
[Control]+[Space]	normal space, non-breaking
[Shift]+[Space]	fixed width space

✦ A non-breaking space ensures that characters either side of it remain together on the same line of text. A fixed width space, unlike a normal space, maintains its width within justified alignments.

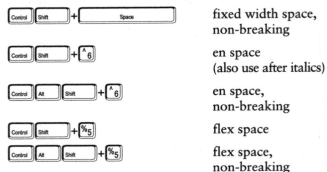

`Control` `Shift` + `Space`	fixed width space, non-breaking
`Control` `Shift` + `^6`	en space (also use after italics)
`Control` `Alt` `Shift` + `^6`	en space, non-breaking
`Control` `Shift` + `%5`	flex space
`Control` `Alt` `Shift` + `%5`	flex space, non-breaking

✦ A flex space is a user-definable space (see page 190).

Page numbers

`Control` + `#3` → page number code

Text commands

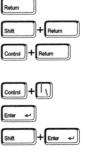

`Return`	paragraph return
`Shift` + `Return`	new line return
`Control` + `Return`	new line return, discretionary
`Control` + `l\`	indent following lines
`Enter ↵`	next column (in text box)
`Shift` + `Enter ↵`	next linked text box

Hyphens and dashes

-	`-.`	hyphen
-	`Control` + `-.`	hyphen, discretionary
–	`Alt` + `+=`	en dash
—	`Control` `Alt` `Shift` + `+=`	em dash

appendix iii

Key work stages

The way you work on documents will be influenced by a number of factors including the nature of the document in hand, the amount of work time you are allocated, the document's importance, personal preferences and such like.

There's no doubt that a structured step-by-step approach to document design and production not only enables you to be more efficient but also allows you to gain the maximum amount of pleasure from working with QuarkXPress.

For these two reasons, I include two typical processes, distilled from the many projects with which I have personally been involved.

The processes are not intended to be a straitjacket; just use them as a guide or checklist and a basis from which to develop processes more suited to your own needs.

Creating documents

Straightforward documents

① Set document size and grid in the New Document dialog box.

② Adjust document preferences, as required.

③ Insert additional document pages, as required.

④ Add ruler guides and items common to *all* document pages to Master A.

⑤ Add ruler guides to document pages.

⑥ Produce page layouts with imported text and scanned images.

⑦ Check spelling, font and picture usage.

⑧ Print pages for evaluation and proofing.

Documents using resources from other documents

① Set document size and grid in the New Document dialog box.

② Adjust document preferences, as required.

③ Insert additional document pages, as required.

④ Add ruler guides and items common to *all* pages to Master A.

⑤ Add ruler guides to document pages.

⑥ Append colours, H&Js and style sheets from other documents in this order.

⑦ Create a library to place frequently-used items.

⑧ Produce page layouts with imported text and scanned images.

⑨ Check spelling, font and picture usage.

⑩ Print pages for evaluation and proof checking.

Creating templates

Stage one

① Set document size and grid in the New Document dialog box.

② Adjust document preferences, as required.

③ Insert additional document pages, as required.

④ Add ruler guides and items common to *all* document pages to Master A.

⑤ Add ruler guides to document pages.

⑥ Create colours, adjust/create additional H&Js.

⑦ Create a library to place frequently-used items.

⑧ Add page items, text and images to individual pages, common to *all* issues.

⑨ Save the document in the usual way. Then Save the document under a different name.

Stage two

① Working on the second 'Saved As' document, produce *sample* page layouts with imported text and scanned images.

② Create style sheets from sample text.

③ Print the sample pages for evaluation and proof checking.

④ Save the document in the usual way. Close the document.

Stage three

① Open the original document.

② Append H&Js and style sheets from the second document in this order.

③ Save the document as a Template under a different name. Close the template.

④ Open the template to work on individual issues.

glossary

absolute page numbers   Numbers which refer to the sequence of pages in a document, starting from the first page.

Adobe Type 1 fonts   PostScript technology used by font manufacturers.

alert box   Dialog box on a screen alerting you to the consequences of a decision you are about to make.

backup   in QuarkXPress, an automatically saved revision of a document.

baseline   Imaginary line on which upper and lower case letters sit; descenders extend below this line.

bitmapped image   Image made up of pixels (or dots).

bromide   Photographic paper used by imagesetters for artwork quality prints.

body   Non-printing height of a font; runs from slightly above ascenders to slightly below descenders.

bit   Smallest possible unit of information; short for binary digit.

bureau   Company specializing in printing and/or imagesetting DTP documents. (In this book, bureau refers also to a repro department at a printing works and a colour copy shop.)

character   Generic name for a letter, number, symbol or 'invisible'.

check box   Small box that works as a toggle for selecting an option. (When you click on an empty box, an X or tick appears, turning it on; when you click again, the X or tick disappears and the option is turned off.).

chooser   Desk accessory used to log into devices, such as printers and other computers linked to a network; also used to enable and disable AppleTalk, Apple's native networking protocol.

clipboard Area of a Macintosh's memory that holds what you last cut or copied; paste inserts a copy of the current contents of the clipboard.

CMYK Stands for cyan, magenta, yellow and key (black), the colour model used in the graphic and printing fields.

column Principal text and image areas, within the page margins.

copyfitting Editing or formatting text to fit within prescribed text areas.

cursor Pointer or other icon indicating the screen position of the mouse.

dialog box Box on a screen requesting information, or a decision, from you.

DTP Short for Desktop Publishing.

drive Floppy, removable or hard disk.

drop cap Large capital letter integrated within the first few lines of a paragraph.

em Measure equal to the width of the square of a font size e.g. a 15 pt em is 15 pt; corresponds roughly the width of a capital M; used as a horizontal unit of measure – *see* en.

en Measure equal to half the width of the square of a font size e.g. a 15 pt en is 7.5 pt; corresponds roughly the width of a lower-case n; used as a horizontal unit of measure – *see* em.

field In QuarkXPress, an area in a dialog box or palette in which you enter values.

film Photographic film used by imagesetters for colour separations.

fixed space Word space which doesn't vary in justified alignments.

flex space User-definable space which doesn't vary in justified alignments.

fold Crease dividing document pages, not to be confused with a bound spine.

folder Sub-division (sub-directory) of a disk.

font Single character – letter, number, punctuation mark or symbol – within a type family. Often used interchangeably with the word 'typeface'.

foundry Company which commissions, designs, makes and markets fonts.

frame Border around a text or picture box; a box rule.

grabber hand   Tool which allows you to move around a document without using the scroll bars.

grayscale   Depiction of grey tones between black and white; usually composed of 256 greys.

greek   Depiction of pictures and text as blocks of grey to speed screen redraw.

grid   Network of column, margin and ruler guides which define the major alignments and principal spaces on a page.

gutter   Vertical space between columns on a page.

half-tone   Pattern (or screen) of dots of different sizes used to simulate a continuous tone photograph, either in colour or monochrome; measured in lines per inch.

H&J   Short for Hyphenation and Justification: a function within QuarkXPress which controls the automatic hyphenation and justification of text within paragraphs.

hyphenation   Breaking of words into two parts to improve word spacing.

I Beam   Pointer's shape when dealing with text.

image   Graphic, photograph or illustration.

imagesetter   Digital phototypesetting machine capable of producing graphic images as well as type on bromide or film (Most imagesetters are PostScript-compatible.).

indent   Set back of lines of text in a paragraph, measured in QuarkXPress from the text box inset.

insertion point   Blinking vertical line indicating where the next keystroke will add or delete text.

invisibles   Characters which don't print, such as ⌷Tab⌷ and ⌷Shift⌷

item   In QuarkXPress, text, picture box or line.

justification   Alignment of text at both sides of a paragraph through the adjustment of word spacing.

kerning   In QuarkXPress, inter-character spacing adjusted either locally or globally; used for styling, and optical reasons.

keystrokes   Use of modifier keys with other keys to execute a command.

keypad   Numeric keys on the right of the keyboard.

leading   Distance between lines of text, usually measured between baselines; measured in points.

line   Printed rule; images which contain black and white areas, without intervening greys.

lpi   Short for lines per inch; the measurement of a half-tone screen

margin   Outer area of the page surrounding the principal text and image areas.

master page   Pages which provide document pages with their column and margin guides.

master page items   Items on document pages provided by master pages.

menu   List of commands.

modifier keys   Keys which modify the effect of a character key: standard modifier keys are [⌘], [Alt], [Shift], [Control] and [Caps Lock].

OPI   Short for Open Press Interface.

orphan   Short line of text at end of paragraph positioned at the top of a column.

orthogonal line   Line which is either horizontal or vertical.

page   One side of a leaf in a document.

palette   Small movable box containing commands.

pantone Matching System   PMS for short; proprietory colour matching system used in the graphics and printing industries.

paragraph   In QuarkXPress, any text separated by ¶.

pasteboard   Temporary storage and work area outside the page, the contents of which don't print out.

photo litho   Short for photo lithography; the primary printing technology used in the printing industry.

PICT   Apple's native file format.

point   Unit of measure; measuring close to $1/72$ inch and very roughly one-third of a millimetre.

process colours   The CMYK colours used to reproduce colour photographs and illustrations.

program   Group of instructions that tells a computer what to do; also called software.

printer   Digital desktop or commercial device for printing or proofing documents primarily using laser, ink jet, die sublimation and thermal wax technologies.

PostScript   Adobe's page description language used by QuarkXPress and other DTP programs.

QuickDraw   Programming routines that enable the Macintosh to display graphic elements on screen; also used to output text and images to certain non-PostScript printers – *see* PostScript.

radio buttons   Group of small buttons for selecting an option, only one of which can be on at any one time.

registration marks   Marks included on film separations for purposes of accurate colour alignment.

remapping   Rearranging the dots within a bitmapped image.

resolution   In this book, the amount of data in a scanned image, measured in pixels (or dots) per linear inch.

RGB   Stands for red, green, blue; the colour model used by monitors and within multimedia documents.

rivers   Unsightly gaps running vertically between words within text.

runaround   In QuarkXPress, the feature which controls the way text is displaced by boxes and images.

running head   Header.

scan   Bitmapped image created by scanner.

scroll bars   Bars equipped with a scroll box and scroll arrows which enable you to scroll vertically or horizontally within windows.

special colour   *See* Spot colour.

spine   Binding edge of a document; part of a document's cover which is visible when placed on a shelf.

spot colour   Colours other than the process colours printed as a separate colour within a photo litho printed document; sometimes called Special colour.

style sheets   Stored grouping of text formats used to format paragraphs quickly and accurately.

system fonts   Fonts which come standard with computers.

template   Document with special content which you use repeatedly; you can modify and/or add to it and save it under a different name but it cannot be accidently overwritten.

TIFF   Short for Tagged Image File Format, the de facto file format for saving scanned images.

tiling   Printing document pages in sections.

tracking   In QuarkXPress, word and letter spacing adjusted either globally or locally; used for copyfitting, styling and to improve readability.

trapping   Technique use to minimize the effects of the mis-registration of photo litho printing on a printed document.

trim marks   Lines printed outside the edge of a document page to indicate the trimmed page size.

truetype fonts   Font technology used for system fonts on both the Macintosh and PCs.

typeface   Collection of letters, numbers, punctuation marks and symbols with an identifiable and consistent appearance. Often used interchangeably with the word 'font'.

typography   Craft of designing with type.

widow   Very short line of text at the end of a paragraph.

window   Enclosed area on the screen in which a document appears.

WP   Short for word processing.

vector image   Drawing or object defined mathematically; sometimes called object orientated.

XTension   Third party program which extends the functionality of QuarkXPress.

Keys

[Alt]   Alt key – a modifier key used in conjunction with other keys, often providing an alternative function; by itself it activates the Grabber Hand

[Delete]   Back space/Delete key – used to delete text to the left of the insertion point, selected text and items

[⌘]   Command key (with an Apple on it) – a modifier key used with other keys to issue commands. By itself it activates the Item tool, when the Content tool is active

[Control]   Control key – a modifier key used in conjunction with other keys. By itself it activates the Zoom tool

[D]   Delete key – used to delete text to the right of the insertion point

[R]   Enter key – used to move text, close dialog boxes and implement field values in the Measurements palette, amongst other things

[Return]   Return key – used to separate paragraphs, close dialog boxes and implement field values in the Measurements palette

[Shift]   Shift key – a modifier key used to capitalize letters and constrain pointer movement, amongst other things

[Tab]   Tab key – keystroke which moves the insertion point to the next tab position, by default 0.5 in apart.

index

teach yourself

Access 2002
moira stephen

- Are you new to Access?
- Do you need support for an IT exam?
- Do you want lots of practice to brush up your skills?

Access 2002 is a comprehensive guide to this database package which is suitable for all beginners. It progresses steadily from basic skills to more advanced features and includes time-saving shortcuts and practical advice.

Moira Stephen is a college lecturer and trainer, specializing in PC applications, and the author of numerous computing books.

Excel 2002
moira stephen

- Are you new to Excel?
- Do you want help with many of the topics commonly found in exams?
- Do you need lots of practice and examples to brush up your skills?

Excel 2002 is a comprehensive guide to this popular package which is suitable for all beginners. It progresses steadily from basic skills to more advanced features and includes time-saving shortcuts and practical advice.

Moira Stephen is a college lecturer and trainer, specializing in PC applications, and the author of numerous computing books.

teach
yourself

Word 2002
moira stephen

- Are you new to Word?
- Do you want help with many topics found in exam syllabuses?
- Do you need lots of practice to brush up your skills?

Word 2002 is a comprehensive guide to this word processing package and is suitable for all beginners. The book progresses from basic skills to more advanced features, with many time-saving shortcuts. Its practical approach, numerous illustrations and guide to automating tasks make it an easy way to brush up your skills.

Moira Stephen is a college lecturer and trainer, specializing in PC applications, and the author of numerous computing books.

the internet
mac bride

- Are you keen to explore the internet with confidence?
- Do you want to get the latest news and information?
- Do you need to do business or go shopping online?

The Internet is a clear, jargon-free introduction for anyone who wants to understand the internet and exploit its rich potential. This book will help you to explore the world wide web, communicate via email, find the information you need, shop or play games online and set up your own home page.

Mac Bride is an IT consultant who has written many top-selling computer programming and applications books.

teach
yourself

html: publishing on the www
mac bride

- Are you an Internet user?
- Do you want to move from browsing to publishing?
- Do you want to explore the possibilities of HTML?

HTML: Publishing on the WWW takes the mysteries out of the
technical issues and jargon of web site building. It covers the
whole of HTML, from the very basics through to style sheets,
clearly explained and with worked examples throughout. With
this book you can learn enough to create a colourful, illustrated
web page in just a few hours, or put together a full-featured,
interactive, interlinked web site in a few days.

Mac Bride is an IT consultant who has written many top-selling
computer programming and applications books.

| teach yourself | **C++**
| | richard riley

- Are you new to programming?
- Do you need to improve your existing C++ skills?
- Do you want to become an expert programmer?

C++ is a concise guide to programming in C++, one of the most popular and versatile languages in use today. All the concepts and techniques you need to create powerful programs are clearly explained, with examples and revision exercises used throughout.

Richard Riley is a computer programmer who has written extensively in C++, Perl, Java, Javascript and HTML.

teach yourself®

Afrikaans
Access 2002
Accounting, Basic
Alexander Technique
Algebra
Arabic
Arabic Script, Beginner's
Aromatherapy
Astronomy
Bach Flower Remedies
Bengali
Better Chess
Better Handwriting
Biology
Body Language
Book Keeping
Book Keeping & Accounting
Brazilian Portuguese
Bridge
Buddhism
Buddhism, 101 Key Ideas
Bulgarian
Business Studies
Business Studies, 101 Key Ideas
C++
Calculus
Calligraphy
Cantonese
Card Games
Catalan
Chemistry, 101 Key Ideas
Chess
Chi Kung
Chinese
Chinese, Beginner's

Chinese Language, Life & Culture
Chinese Script, Beginner's
Christianity
Classical Music
Copywriting
Counselling
Creative Writing
Crime Fiction
Croatian
Crystal Healing
Czech
Danish
Desktop Publishing
Digital Photography
Digital Video & PC Editing
Drawing
Dream Interpretation
Dutch
Dutch, Beginner's
Dutch Dictionary
Dutch Grammar
Eastern Philosophy
ECDL
E-Commerce
Economics, 101 Key Ideas
Electronics
English, American (EFL)
English as a Foreign Language
English, Correct
English Grammar
English Grammar (EFL)
English, Instant, for French Speakers
English, Instant, for German Speakers
English, Instant, for Italian Speakers
English, Instant, for Spanish Speakers

English for International Business
English Language, Life & Culture
English Verbs
English Vocabulary
Ethics
Excel 2002
Feng Shui
Film Making
Film Studies
Finance for non-Financial Managers
Finnish
Flexible Working
Flower Arranging
French
French, Beginner's
French Grammar
French Grammar, Quick Fix
French, Instant
French, Improve your
French Language, Life & Culture
French Starter Kit
French Verbs
French Vocabulary
Gaelic
Gaelic Dictionary
Gardening
Genetics
Geology
German
German, Beginner's
German Grammar
German Grammar, Quick Fix
German, Instant
German, Improve your
German Language, Life & Culture
German Verbs
German Vocabulary
Go
Golf
Greek
Greek, Ancient
Greek, Beginner's
Greek, Instant
Greek, New Testament
Greek Script, Beginner's
Guitar
Gulf Arabic
Hand Reflexology
Hebrew, Biblical
Herbal Medicine
Hieroglyphics
Hindi
Hindi, Beginner's
Hindi Script, Beginner's

Hinduism
History, 101 Key Ideas
How to Win at Horse Racing
How to Win at Poker
HTML Publishing on the WWW
Human Anatomy & Physiology
Hungarian
Icelandic
Indian Head Massage
Indonesian
Information Technology, 101 Key Ideas
Internet, The
Irish
Islam
Italian
Italian, Beginner's
Italian Grammar
Italian Grammar, Quick Fix
Italian, Instant
Italian, Improve your
Italian Language, Life & Culture
Italian Verbs
Italian Vocabulary
Japanese
Japanese, Beginner's
Japanese, Instant
Japanese Language, Life & Culture
Japanese Script, Beginner's
Java
Jewellery Making
Judaism
Korean
Latin
Latin American Spanish
Latin, Beginner's
Latin Dictionary
Latin Grammar
Letter Writing Skills
Linguistics
Linguistics, 101 Key Ideas
Literature, 101 Key Ideas
Mahjong
Managing Stress
Marketing
Massage
Mathematics
Mathematics, Basic
Media Studies
Meditation
Mosaics
Music Theory
Needlecraft
Negotiating
Nepali

Norwegian
Origami
Panjabi
Persian, Modern
Philosophy
Philosophy of Mind
Philosophy of Religion
Philosophy of Science
Philosophy, 101 Key Ideas
Photography
Photoshop
Physics
Piano
Planets
Planning Your Wedding
Polish
Politics
Portuguese
Portuguese, Beginner's
Portuguese Grammar
Portuguese, Instant
Portuguese Language, Life & Culture
Postmodernism
Pottery
Powerpoint 2002
Presenting for Professionals
Project Management
Psychology
Psychology, 101 Key Ideas
Psychology, Applied
Quark Xpress
Quilting
Recruitment
Reflexology
Reiki
Relaxation
Retaining Staff
Romanian
Russian
Russian, Beginner's
Russian Grammar
Russian, Instant
Russian Language, Life & Culture
Russian Script, Beginner's
Sanskrit
Screenwriting
Serbian
Setting up a Small Business
Shorthand, Pitman 2000
Sikhism
Spanish
Spanish, Beginner's
Spanish Grammar
Spanish Grammar, Quick Fix

Spanish, Instant
Spanish, Improve your
Spanish Language, Life & Culture
Spanish Starter Kit
Spanish Verbs
Spanish Vocabulary
Speaking on Special Occasions
Speed Reading
Statistical Research
Statistics
Swahili
Swahili Dictionary
Swedish
Tagalog
Tai Chi
Tantric Sex
Teaching English as a Foreign Language
Teaching English One to One
Teams and Team-Working
Thai
Time Management
Tracing your Family History
Travel Writing
Trigonometry
Turkish
Turkish, Beginner's
Typing
Ukrainian
Urdu
Urdu Script, Beginner's
Vietnamese
Volcanoes
Watercolour Painting
Weight Control through Diet and
    Exercise
Welsh
Welsh Dictionary
Welsh Language, Life & Culture
Wills and Probate
Wine Tasting
Winning at Job Interviews
Word 2002
World Faiths
Writing a Novel
Writing for Children
Writing Poetry
Xhosa
Yoga
Zen
Zulu

available from bookshops and on-line retailers